KARATEDO KATA MODEL

空手道形教範

第一指定形

サイファ
SAIFA

セーパイ
SEIPAI

ジオン
JION

カンクウダイ
KANKUDAI

for TEACHING

バッサイダイ
BASSAIDAI

セイエンチン
SEIENCHIN

セイシャン
SEISHAN

チントウ
CHINTO

DAIICHI SHITEIGATA

公益財団法人全日本空手道連盟
JAPAN KARATEDO FEDERATION

序文

公益財団法人全日本空手道連盟

会長 笹川 堯

　私たち公益財団法人全日本空手道連盟は、空手道を通して技と心を修練する姿を、「礼」と「節」の精神を基盤とするところであり、「礼」とは、人を敬い人に感謝し、社会秩序を保つ理念であり、「節」とは、善悪の判断ができ、自己を律する節度であります。この精神を規範として心身のバランスのとれた人間形成に至る大事な側面をしっかりと支え、教育実践に寄与するものであります。

　全空連では、正しい形の継承と普及を目的として１９８２年（昭和57年）に中央技術委員会より８つの形を指定形として「空手道形教範」を刊行致しましたが、この度「空手道形教範　第一指定形」を新たに刊行する運びとなりました。空手道の正しい伝統形の指導および継承、公式競技会や公認段位審査における形の評価基準の統一を図ったものであります。

　このことによって、空手道の形指導書に関しては、「空手道形教範　基本形」、「空手道形教範　第一指定形」、さらに「空手道形教範　第二指定形」が完全整備されたことになります。

　指導者においてはこれらの「空手道形教範」を有効活用され、形指導についての一層の理解を深められるとともに、充実した空手道指導にあたられることを心から期待いたします。

平成２９年１０月

Preface

Japan Karatedo Federation

President Takashi Sasagawa

Our national association, Japan Karatedo Federation, is founded on the principles of 'Rei', or manners, and 'Setsu', or integrity, as a means to train the body and mind through Karatedo. "Rei" is a means of showing respect and gratitude towards people, as well as maintaining social order. "Setsu" is being able to judge right from wrong, and having good self-discipline. Through adhering to this standard, JKF endorses aspects of human development that are both mentally and physically balanced, and contribute towards their implementation in education.

For the purpose of passing on and propagating the correct way of performing Kata, in 1982 the JKF central technical committee published the first edition of the book "Karatedo Kata Model for Teaching" for 8 designated, or 'Shitei', kata. Now, we are ready to introduce the latest edition, now called "Karatedo Kata Model for Teaching Dai-Ichi Shiteigata". This guide provides readers with correct traditional forms to pass on for use in Kata instruction, as well as integrateing required criteria for grade assessment and competition.

Subsequently, the first book resulted in the publication of a series of instruction guides: "Karatedo Kata Model for Teaching Dai-Ichi Shiteigata", "Karatedo Kata Model for Teaching Dai-Ni Shiteigata", and "Karatedo Kata Model for Teaching Kihon Kata".

I sincerely hope that this book will be used effectively by instructors to deepen their understanding of kata, as well as help provide enriched guidance with their own teaching.

October, 2017

もくじ

序文　笹川　堯	・・・・・・・・・・・・・	2
もくじ	・・・・・・・・・・・・・	4
サイファ　SAIFA	・・・・・・・・・・・・・	7
セーパイ　SEIPAI	・・・・・・・・・・・	27
ジオン　JION	・・・・・・・・・・・	51
カンクウダイ　KANKUDAI	・・・・・・・・・・・・・	81
バッサイダイ　BASSAIDAI	・・・・・・・・・・・・・	121
セイエンチン　SEIENCHIN	・・・・・・・・・・・・	151
セイシャン　SEISHAN	・・・・・・・・・・・・	179
チントウ　CHINTO	・・・・・・・・・・・・・	205

サイファ
SAIFA

特徴

サイファは短かい形であるが立ち方の種類が多く、また剛柔流の特徴のある技が多く含まれている。
各立ち方の正確さと移動のスムーズさが求められ、手技とのバランスが大切である。

Though being a short Kata, SAIFA contains various types of stances, as well as major techniques of the Goju-ryu style. Smoothness of movements, precise techniques, as well as balance are emphasized.

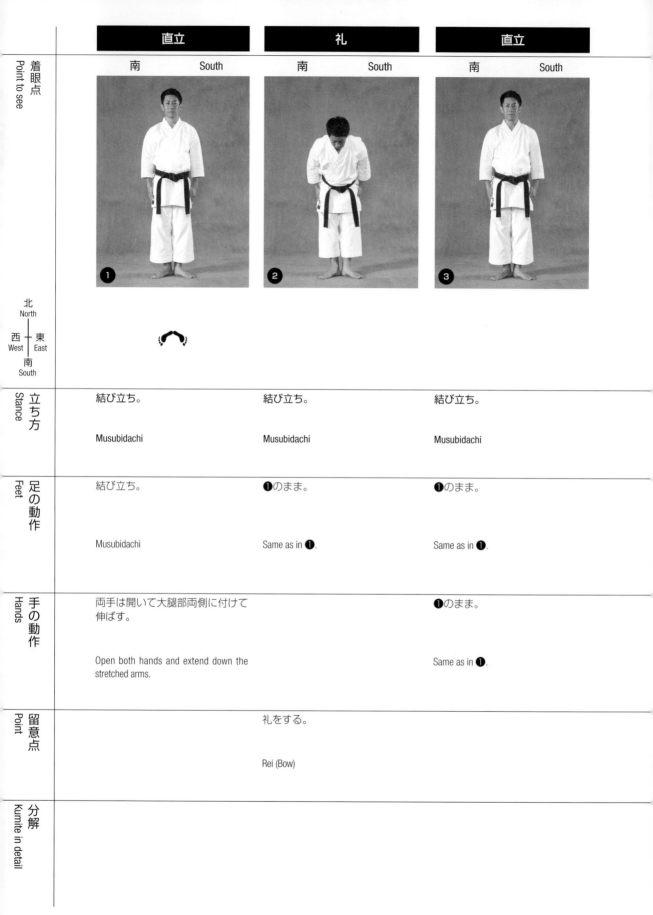

8　サイファ　SAIFA

	用意	1 挙動	
	南（正面やや高め）South (slightly upward)	南　　　South	東　　　East

結び立ち。	平行立ち。	結び立ち。
Musubidachi	Heikodachi	Musubidachi
❶のまま。	両上足底を軸に平行立ちとなる。	右足を南西の方向に1歩進め、左足を引きつけ東向き、結び立ちとなる。
Same as in ❶.	Pivoting on the balls of the feet, slide heels out until parallel.	Take right foot one step toward southwest, then, pulling left foot together, face east to stand Musubidachi.
両手を開き下腹部前に構える（左手前、右手後ろ）。	両手を握りながら両体側へ手の甲を外側に構える。	右縦拳を右脇にあげ、左手は縦拳部を握る。
Open both hands and place them in front of the lower abdomen, with the left hand over right.	Clenching the fists, move them to the sides of the body, with back of the hand facing outwards.	Lift Right-Tateken up to right armpit, grasp Right-Tateken with left hand.
呼吸は「短呑」。	呼吸は「長吐」。膝が伸び、棒立ちにならないよう注意。	移動は摺り足で、腰が上下しないようにする。
Breath Tan-don (inhale briefly).	Breath Cho-to (Exhale deeply). Pay attention that knees do not stand upright.	Move with a sliding step while avoiding up and down movements of the hips.

写真❺〜❿の分解　　SAIFA Kumite in detail

2 挙動

	東　　　East	南（体は東）　South (body faces east)
着眼点 Point to see	途中  ❽  東から見る ❽ seen from east.	 ❿  東から見る ❿ seen from east. ⓫
立ち方 Stance	結び立ち。 Musubidachi	四股立ち。 Shikodachi
足の動作 Feet	❻のまま。 Same as in ❻.	左足を北の方向に引き、四股立ちとなる。 Pull left foot back toward north to stand Shikodachi.
手の動作 Hands	❻が終わると同時に左手は右拳を握ったまま右拳を左乳下へ振りきるように移動させる。 As soon as finishing ❻, while left hand clasping right fist, swing right fist with force toward lower left side of the breast.	右上段裏拳打ち。左手は顔面辺りから指先を上に水月の前に構える（押え受け）。 Right-Jyodan-Uraken-Uchi. With fingers pointing upward, move left hand from around the height of face to front of solar plexus (Osaeuke).
留意点 Point	左に寄せる時、力強く素早くする。 右前腕を体から1拳分離す。 When drawing hands to the left, move quickly and forcefully. Hold the right arm one fist's breadth from the body.	裏拳打ちは素早く引き戻す。手首がしっかり返っているか注意（スナップ）。 Pull the Uraken strike back quickly by snapping the wrist.
分解 Kumite in detail		

10　サイファ　SAIFA

3挙動

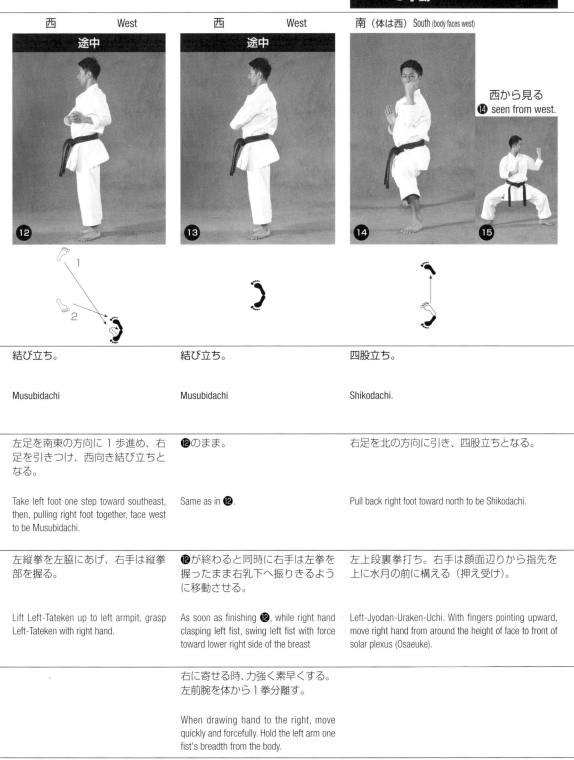

西 West 途中 ⓬	西 West 途中 ⓭	南（体は西）South (body faces west) ⓮ 西から見る ⓮ seen from west. ⓯
結び立ち。	結び立ち。	四股立ち。
Musubidachi	Musubidachi	Shikodachi.
左足を南東の方向に１歩進め、右足を引きつけ、西向き結び立ちとなる。	⓬のまま。	右足を北の方向に引き、四股立ちとなる。
Take left foot one step toward southeast, then, pulling right foot together, face west to be Musubidachi.	Same as in ⓬.	Pull back right foot toward north to be Shikodachi.
左縦拳を左脇にあげ、右手は縦拳部を握る。	⓬が終わると同時に右手は左拳を握ったまま右乳下へ振りきるように移動させる。	左上段裏拳打ち。右手は顔面辺りから指先を上に水月の前に構える（押え受け）。
Lift Left-Tateken up to left armpit, grasp Left-Tateken with right hand.	As soon as finishing ⓬, while right hand clasping left fist, swing left fist with force toward lower right side of the breast	Left-Jyodan-Uraken-Uchi. With fingers pointing upward, move right hand from around the height of face to front of solar plexus (Osaeuke).
	右に寄せる時、力強く素早くする。左前腕を体から１拳分離す。	
	When drawing hand to the right, move quickly and forcefully. Hold the left arm one fist's breadth from the body.	

4 挙動

	東　　East	東　　East	南（体は東）　South(body faces east)
着眼点 Point to see	途中 ⓰	途中 ⓱	⓲
立ち方 Stance	結び立ち。 Musubidachi	結び立ち。 Musubidachi	四股立ち。 Shikodachi
足の動作 Feet	右足を南西の方向に1歩進め、左足を引きつけ東向き、結び立ちとなる。 Take right foot one step toward southwest, then, pulling left foot together, face east to stand Musubidachi.	⓰のまま。 Same as in ⓰.	左足を北の方向に引き、四股立ちとなる。 Pull left foot back toward north to stand Shikodachi.
手の動作 Hands	右縦拳を右脇にあげ、左手は縦拳部を握る。 Lift Right-Tateken up to right armpit, grasp Right-Tateken with left hand.	⓰が終わると同時に左手は右拳を握ったまま右拳を左乳下へ振りきるように移動させる。 As soon as finishing ⓰, while left hand clasping right fist, swing right fist with force toward lower left side of the breast.	右上段裏拳打ち。左手は顔面辺りから指先を上に水月の前に構える（押え受け）。 Right-Jyodan-Uraken-Uchi. With fingers pointing upward, move left hand from around the height of face to front of solar plexus (Osaeuke).
留意点 Point			
分解 Kumite in detail			

12　サイファ　SAIFA

西（体は南） West (body faces south)	南　　　　South	南　　　　South

⑲　　　　　　　　　　　　⑳　　　　　　　　　　　　㉑

左片足立ち。	左片足立ち。
Standing on the left leg.	Standing on the left leg.
左足を右足の東の方向へ１歩出し、右膝当て。右足爪先を下げる。	右膝当て（⑲）より右中段前蹴り。
Step towards the east with left foot, execute Right-Hizaate. Point the right foot's toes downward.	Right-Hizaate (as in ⑲), then, Right-Chudan-Maegeri.
左中段すくい掛け受け（開掌）、右下段押え受け（開掌）。	⑲のまま。
Left-Chudan-Sukui-Kakeuke with Kaisho. Right-Gedan-Osaeuke with Kaisho.	Same as in ⑲.
膝当てをする足は、爪先を下げる。	蹴る瞬間南を向く。
Point the raised foot's toes downward.	Face toward south at the moment of kick.

写真⑲〜⑳の分解　　SAIFA Kumite in detail

	東（体は南）　East (body faces south)	南　　　South	南　　　South
着眼点 Point to see	途中 ㉒	途中 ㉓	途中 ㉔
立ち方 Stance	右片足立ち。 Standing on the right leg.	右片足立ち。 Standing on the right leg.	右前屈立ち。 Right-Zenkutsudachi.
足の動作 Feet	右足を左足の西の方向へ1歩出し、左膝当て。左足爪先を下げる。 Taking right foot one step toward west of left foot, execute Left-Hizaate.Point the left foot's toes downward.	左膝当て（㉒）より左中段前蹴り。 Left-Hizaate (as in ㉒), then, Left-Chudan-Maegeri.	蹴った左足を北の方向に引き、右足前、前屈立ちとなる。 After kicking, pull back left foot toward north.
手の動作 Hands	右中段すくい掛け受け（開掌）、左下段押え受け（開掌）。 Right-Chudan-Sukui-Kakeuke with Kaisho. Left-Gedan-Osaeuke with Kaisho.	㉒のまま。 Same as in ㉒.	開掌の両手は握りながら甲を上に両脇に引きつける。 Clench both fists with the back of the hand facing upward, and pull in to the sides.
留意点 Point	膝当てをする足は、爪先を下げる。 Point the raised foot's toes downward.	蹴る瞬間南を向く。 Face toward south at the moment of kick.	
分解 Kumite in detail			

北 North
西 West ／ 東 East
南 South

14　サイファ　SAIFA

5 挙動

南　　　South	南　　　South	
 ㉕	 ㉖	 ㉗

右前屈立ち。	右前屈立ち。	
Right-Zenkutsudachi.	Right-Zenkutsudachi.	
㉔のまま。	㉔のまま。	右足を東へ、左足の前を通り交差させる。
Same as in ㉔.	Same as in ㉔.	Move the right foot towards east, crossing in front of the left foot.
肩よりやや高く、肩幅よりやや広く正拳両手突き。	両拳は半円を描くように右拳は拳槌。左拳は開きながら体の中心部前、右膝上縦拳で2つ位の高さ辺りを打つ。	
Execute Seiken-Morotetsuki, aiming slightly above shoulder height and slightly outside shoulder width.	Draw a semi-circle with both hands and execute Right-Kentsui striking the open left palm at a position in the front center of the body at a height of two Tateken higher than knee level.	
	左右の手は肘関節を支点に前腕部だけで円を描くように回す（両肘を軸に）。	
	Both hands turn like drawing a circle fulcruming joint of elbow (making elbows axis).	

写真㉕〜㉖の分解　　SAIFA Kumite in detail

		北　　North	北　　North
着眼点 Point to see	㉙の直前を北から見る ㉗ to ㉙ seen from north. **28** 北 North 西 — 東 West — East 南 South	途中 **29**	途中 **30**
立ち方 Stance		左前屈立ち。 Left-Zenkutsudachi.	左前屈立ち。 Left-Zenkutsudachi.
足の動作 Feet		すかさず体を左回転させて北の方向を向く。 Without pause, quickly rotate the body left to face North.	㉙のまま。 Same as in ㉙.
手の動作 Hands		左掛け受けをしながら甲を上に両拳を両脇に引きつける。 Execute Left-Kakeuke and pull both fists in to the sides, with the back of the hand facing upward.	肩よりやや高く、肩幅よりやや広く正拳両手突き。 Execute Seiken-Morotetsuki, aiming slightly above shoulder height and slightly outside shoulder width.
留意点 Point		【備考】㉔の左右反対の体勢。 <Note>Reverse of ㉔.	【備考】㉕の左右反対動作。 <Note>Reverse of ㉕.
分解 Kumite in detail		写真㉛の分解　　　*SAIFA Kumite in detail*	

16 サイファ　SAIFA

6 挙動

北　North　　　　　　　　　　　　　　　南（体は東）South (body faces east)

東から見る
❸ seen from east.

左前屈立ち。		平行立ち。
Left-Zenkutsudachi.		Heikoudachi
㉙のまま。	右足は内側に足払い、体を東の方向に回転させる。	平行立ちとなる。
Same as in ㉙.	Execute Ashibarai with right foot to the inside, and, using the momentum, rotate body toward east.	Move into Heikoudachi
両拳は半円を描くように左拳は拳槌、右拳は開きながら体の中心部、左膝上縦拳で2つ位の高さ辺りを打つ。 Draw a semi-circle with both hands and end with Left-Kentsui striking the open right palm at a position in the front center of the body at a height two Tateken higher than knee level.		右上段拳槌打ち。頭頂部を通る。左拳は脇に構える。 Right-Jodan-Kentsuiuchi. Aim to strike down the head. Hold the left fist at the left side.
【備考】㉖の左右反対動作。 <Note>Reverse of ㉖.		着地と拳鎚打ちが同時になるようにする。気合を掛ける。拳鎚の位置は額の高さ。 Ensure that the strike and the foot land simultaneously, with 'Kiai'. Strike the top of the opponent's head.

Point to see 着眼点	**7 挙動**	

南（体は東） South (body faces east)

東から見る
㉟ seen from east.

途中

北 North
西 West ／ 東 East
南 South

Stance 立ち方

平行立ち。

Heikoudachi

Feet 足の動作

㉝のまま。

Same as in ㉝.

左足は内側に足払い。

Execute Ashibarai with left foot to the inside.

Hands 手の動作

右拳槌はその位置で手の甲を上にして開掌、その開掌を指先に力を入れながら右脇に引く。左拳は中段裏突き。

Keeping the right fist in the same position, open up into Kaishou with the back of the hand facing upward. Tensing up to the fingertips, pull the right hand back to the right side of the body. The left hand executes Chudan-Uratsuki.

Point 留意点

体は東のまま腰を使い、裏突きをする。
左肩を前に出さない。

Keep the body facing right and use the hips to execute Uratsuki. Be sure not to move the left shoulder forward.

Kumite in detail 分解

写真㉜～㉟の分解   *SAIFA Kumite in detail*

18 サイファ　SAIFA

8 挙動

北（体は東） North (body faces east)

途中

東から見る
❸ seen from east.

北（体は東） North (body faces east)

東から見る
❹ seen from east.

平行立ち。	平行立ち。
Heikoudachi	Heikoudachi
平行立ちとなる。	❸のまま。
Move into Heikoudachi.	Same as in ❸.
左上段拳槌打ち。頭頂部を通る。右拳は脇に構える。	左拳槌はその位置で手の甲を上にして開掌、その開掌を指先に力を入れながら左脇に引く。右拳は中段裏突き。
Left-Jodan-Kentsuiuchi. Aim to strike down the head. Hold the right fist at the right side.	Keeping the left fist in the same position, open up into Kaishou with the back of the hand facing upward. Tensing up to the fingertips, pull the left hand back to the left side of the body. The right hand executes Chudan Uratsuki.
着地と拳槌打ちが同時になるようにする。 気合を掛ける。 拳槌の位置は額の高さ。 Ensure that the strike and the foot land simultaneously, with 'Kiai'. Strike the top of the opponent's head.	右肩を前に出さない。 Be sure not to move the right shoulder forward.

19

		9 挙動	

北　　　North

途中

北から見る
❷ seen from north.

北　　　North

北から見る
❹ seen from north.

北
North

西 ─ 東
West East

南
South

着眼点 Point to see			
立ち方 Stance	右三戦立ち。 Right-Sanchindachi	右三戦立ち。 Right-Sanchindachi	
足の動作 Feet	右足を北の方向に進め、右三戦立ち。 Step right foot forward to north.	❷のまま。 Same as in ❷.	
手の動作 Hands		左拳は甲を上にした構えより肩の高さへ正拳突き。右拳は脇に構える。 Keeping back of hand facing upward, execute Chudan-Seikentsuki with left fist toward shoulder height level. Hold right fist under right armpit.	
留意点 Point			
分解 Kumite in detail			

20　サイファ　SAIFA

北 North	南 South	南 South
	右猫足立ち。	右猫足立ち。
	Right-Nekoashidachi	Right-Nekoashidachi
左足を右足前（北）へ１歩踏み出す。	体を右に半回転（180°）させて右猫足立ちとなる。	㊼のまま。
Move the left foot one step in front of the right, to the North.	Rotate the body 180 degrees to the right, into Right-Nekoashidachi.	Same as in ㊼.
	左手は掌を上にして左脇に構える（開掌）。右手は背刀打ち、左開掌の上に構える。	
	Hold the left hand to the side of the body with the palm facing upward. Execute right Haito-Uchi, and hold it above the left hand.	

写真㊼の分解　　SAIFA Kumite in detail

		10 挙動		

		南　　　　South	南　　　　South	南　　　　South
着眼点 Point to see		途中 ㊾	 ㊿	途中 51
		北 North 西—東 West　East 南 South		
立ち方 Stance		右猫足立ち。 Right-Nekoashidachi	右猫足立ち。 Right-Nekoashidachi	右猫足立ち。 Right-Nekoashidachi
足の動作 Feet		㊼のまま。 Same as in ㊼.	㊼のまま。 Same as in ㊼.	㊼のまま。 Same as in ㊼.
手の動作 Hands		左右回し受け。右手は上より円を描くように指先を下に向け右脇に構える。左手は脇の位置で回し指先を上に向けて左脇に構える。 Execute Mawashiuke with both hands, by drawing right hand as if making a circle in front of face and bring it under right armpit, with fingers pointing down ward. At the same time, point the fingers of the left hand upward by twisting the wrist clockwise with fingers pointing upward.	左手は指先を上、掌底で大胸筋、右掌底で鼠蹊部を押す。 Press Left Shotei to the opponent's chest (left side), with the fingers facing upward, while pressing the groin with the right Shotei	
留意点 Point			両掌とも、出来るだけ正面に向ける。 Both palms face front as much as possible.	
分解 Kumite in detail				

22　サイファ　SAIFA

	11 挙動	止め（直立）
南 South 	南 South 	南 South 
	結び立ち。 Musubidachi	結び立ち。 Musubidachi
	右足を左足に引きつける。 Pull right foot to left foot until heels come together.	❸のまま。 Same as in ❸.
	両手は右掌を上、左掌を下に重ね、回すように下腹部前に重ねて構える（左手前、右手後ろ）。 With the right palm at the top, place the hands together and bring inward to the body, then moving them to in front of the lower abdomen, plams down, with the left hand over right.	両手は開いて大腿部両側に付けて伸ばす。 Open both hands and stretch both sides of thighs.

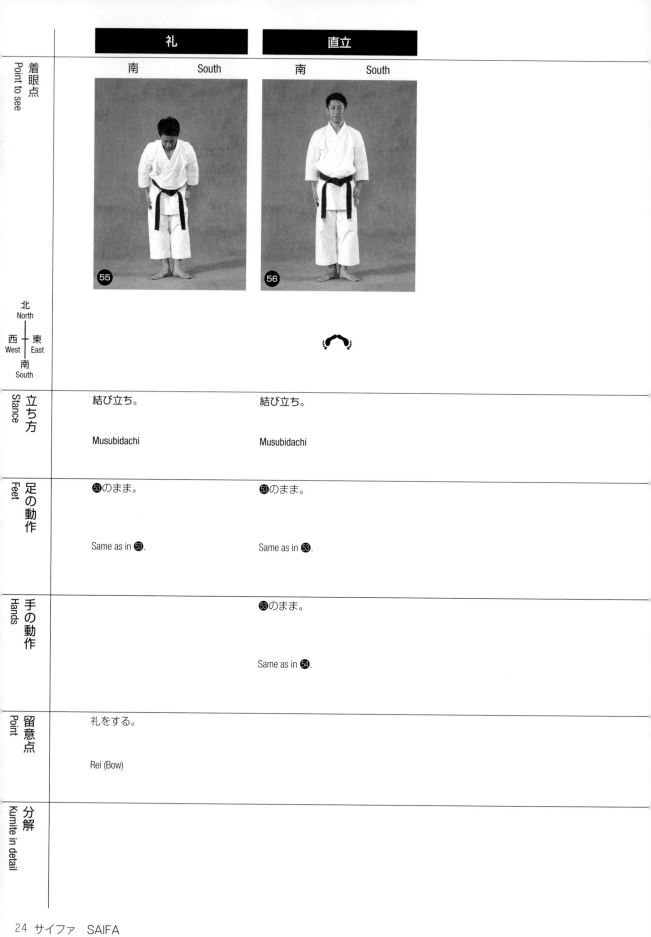

	礼	直立
着眼点 Point to see	南 South	南 South
立ち方 Stance	結び立ち。 Musubidachi	結び立ち。 Musubidachi
足の動作 Feet	❸のまま。 Same as in ❸.	❸のまま。 Same as in ❸.
手の動作 Hands		❸のまま。 Same as in ❹.
留意点 Point	礼をする。 Rei (Bow)	
分解 Kumite in detail		

24 サイファ SAIFA

サイファ

セーパイ

ジオン

カンクウダイ

バッサイダイ

セイエンチン

セイシャン

チントウ

25

セーパイ

SEIPAI

特徴

セーパイは逆技・投げ技など接近戦での護身術として効果的な技が多い。特に巧妙な円の動きが特徴である。攻防技が一連になっていて緩急の動作をリズミカルにすることが求められる。

SEIPAI has plenty of effective techniques for self-defense in Sekkin-Sen such as reversal and throwing techniques. A special characteristic of SEIPAI is the use of circular movements in it techniques. It is necessary that defensive and offensive techniques flow rhythmically from one to the other.

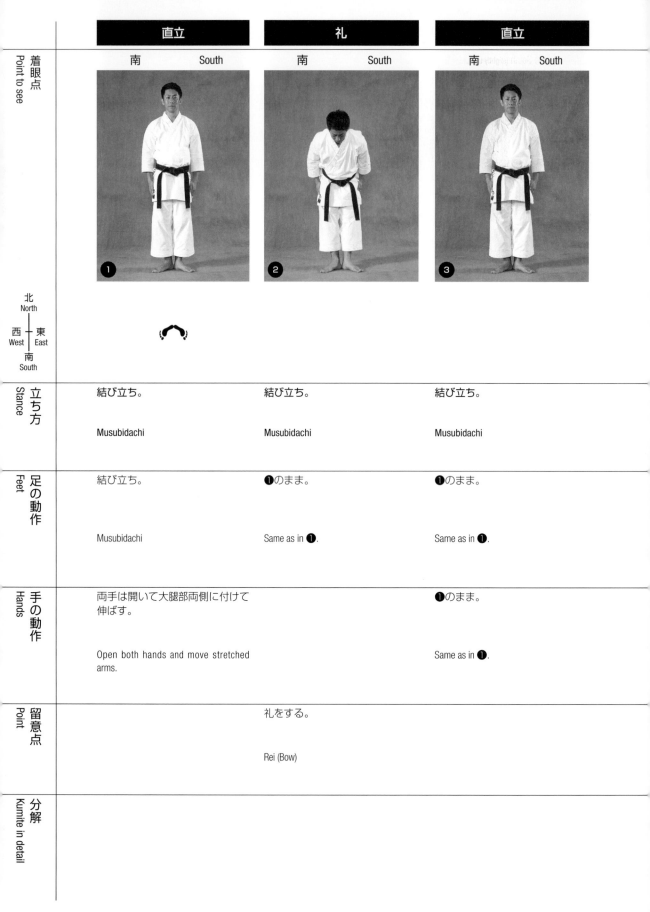

用意	1 挙動	2 挙動
南（正面やや高め）South (slightly upward)	南　　　South	南　　　South
		 seen from east.
結び立ち。 Musubidachi	平行立ち。 Heikodachi	四股立ち。 Shikodachi
❶のまま。 Same as in ❶.	両上足底を軸に平行立ちとなる。 Pivoting on the balls of the feet, slide heels out until parallel.	左足を北の方向に引いて四股立ちとなる。 Pull left foot back toward north, then, Shikodachi.
両手を開き下腹部前に構える（左手前、右手後ろ）。 Open both hands and place them in front of the lower abdomen, with the left hand over right.	両手を握りながら両体側へ手の甲を外側に構える。 Clenching the fists, move them to the sides, with the back of the hand facing outwards.	左開掌。指先を上に顔の前で半円を描きながら水月の前で構える。並行して右縦貫手は左腕の内側から上より半円を描くように南方向に腕を目の高さに伸ばす。肘に余裕を持たせる。 With left hand in Kaisho and the fingers pointing upward, draw a semicircle up to in front of the face, then lower and hold in front of solar plexus. At the same time draw a semicircle with the right hand, from the inside of the left arm, up and then down towards South. Keep the elbows relaxed.
呼吸は「短呑」。 Breath Tan-don (inhale briefly).	呼吸は「長吐」。 膝が伸び、棒立ちにならないよう注意。 Breath Cho-to (Exhale deeply). Pay attention that knees do not stand upright.	四股立ち。腰が高く両膝が内にしぼんでしまわないようにする。 Shikodachi:Do not stand up with high hip position and avoid inward twisting the knees.

写真❺〜❻の分解　　SEIPAI Kumite in detail

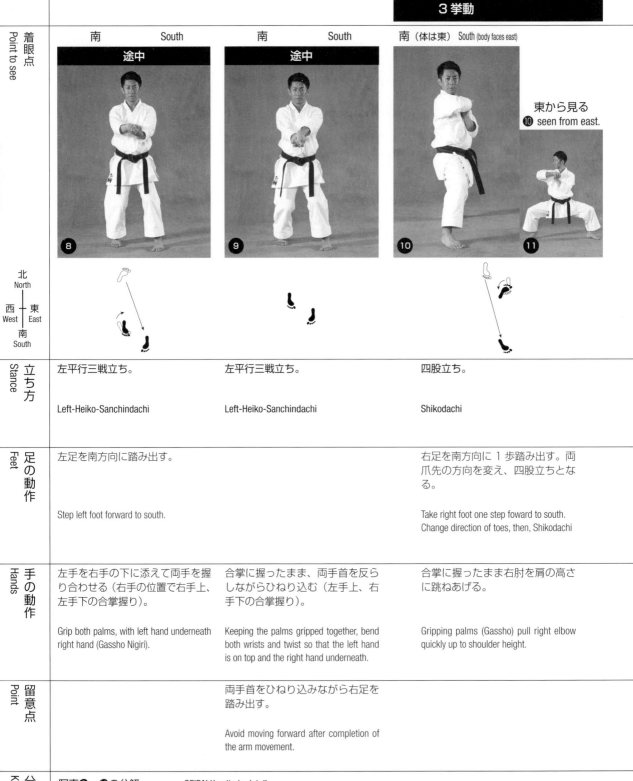

Point to see 着眼点	南 South 途中 ❽	南 South 途中 ❾	南（体は東）South (body faces east) ❿	東から見る ❿ seen from east. ⓫
Stance 立ち方	左平行三戦立ち。 Left-Heiko-Sanchindachi	左平行三戦立ち。 Left-Heiko-Sanchindachi	四股立ち。 Shikodachi	
Feet 足の動作	左足を南方向に踏み出す。 Step left foot forward to south.		右足を南方向に１歩踏み出す。両爪先の方向を変え、四股立ちとなる。 Take right foot one step foward to south. Change direction of toes, then, Shikodachi	
Hands 手の動作	左手を右手の下に添えて両手を握り合わせる（右手の位置で右手上、左手下の合掌握り）。 Grip both palms, with left hand underneath right hand (Gassho Nigiri).	合掌に握ったまま、両手首を反らしながらひねり込む（左手上、右手下の合掌握り）。 Keeping the palms gripped together, bend both wrists and twist so that the left hand is on top and the right hand underneath.	合掌に握ったまま右肘を肩の高さに跳ねあげる。 Gripping palms (Gassho) pull right elbow quickly up to shoulder height.	
Point 留意点		両手首をひねり込みながら右足を踏み出す。 Avoid moving forward after completion of the arm movement.		
Kumite in detail 分解	写真❽～❿の分解　　SEIPAI Kumite in detail 			

30　セーパイ　SEIPAI

4 挙動

南（体は西）　South (body faces west)

西から見る
⓬ seen from west.

⓬　⓭

南（体は西）　South (body faces west)

途中

西から見る
⓮ seen from west.

⓮　⓯

後屈立ち。

Kokutsudachi (left foot in front).

後屈立ち。

Kokutsudachi

左足を南方向に出し、左足前、後屈立ちとなる。

Step left foot forward to south.

⓬のまま。

Same as in ⓬.

左開掌にて腕を体の線に平行になるように伸ばし、下段掌底当て、右肘は肩より高くあげ、腕、掌を伸ばし、体の線に平行になるように下に向ける。

Left hand Kaisho, stretch left arm parallel to the side, executing Gedan-Shoteiate. Pull right elbow higher than shoulder height, with arm and palm facing downward, stretch parallel to center line of the body.

右手はそのまま。左手は左中段裏受けをする。

Right hand same as in ⓬. Left hand executes Chudan Urauke.

左手は右手の内側より円を描きながら下段掌底当てをする。

Left hand Gedan-Shoteiate after making an arc from inside of right hand.

写真⓬の分解　　SEIPAI Kumite in detail

31

着眼点 Point to see	南　　　　South	南　　　　South	南（体は西）South (body faces west)
	途中	途中	途中　　　　　　西から見る ⑱ seen from west.
	⑯	⑰	⑱　　　⑲

北 North　西 West　東 East　南 South

立ち方 Stance	左半前屈立ち。 Left-Half-Zenkutsudachi	左片足立ち。 Standing on left leg.	四股立ち。 Shikodachi
足の動作 Feet	両足を軸に南方向に半前屈になるよう、体の向きを変える。 Pivoting on both balls of the feet, shift body direction toward south.	右中段前蹴り。 Right Chudan-Maegeri.	右足を北方向に引き、四股立ちとなる。 Pull down right foot toward north, then, Shikodachi.
手の動作 Hands	右上段手刀外回し打ち。左開掌は掌を前向に左脇に揃える。 Jyodan side blow attack with right Shuto. Left hand Kaisho, with palm facing forward, hold it under left armpit.	⑯のまま。 Same as in ⑯.	左中段回し肘当ての動作。右後ろ肘当て。 Left-Chudan-Mawashi-Hijiate (elbow strike) movement. The right elbow strikes behind.
留意点 Point	左手首がまっすぐにならないようにする（手首で相手攻撃を押さえる）。 Left wrist must not straighten without bending (press down opponent's attack with wrist).	左手が脇から離れないよう注意。 Do not separate left hand from the body.	左手が前方に出ないよう注意。 Take care not to let the elbow out too far in front.
分解 Kumite in detail	写真⑭〜⑰の分解　　SEIPAI Kumite in detail		

32　セーパイ　SEIPAI

5 挙動

南（体は西）　South (body faces west)

西から見る
⑳ seen from west.

北　　　　North

途中

北から見る
㉒ seen from north.

四股立ち。	右猫足立ち。
Shikodachi	Right-Nekoashidachi
⑱のまま。	左足を軸に体を90°回転、北方向を向き、右足を寄せて右猫足立ちとなる。
Same as in ⑱.	Pivoting on left foot, turn body 90 degree toward north and pull right foot into Right-Nekoashidachi.
左上段裏拳打ち。右拳は脇に引いたまま。	右拳は下段受け、左拳は甲を上に右肘の下に構える。
Left-Jyodan-Uraken-Uchi. Right fist remains the same.	Right-Gedan-Uke. Hold left fist under right elbow with back of hand facing upward.

写真⑱〜⑳の分解　　*SEIPAI Kumite in detail*

33

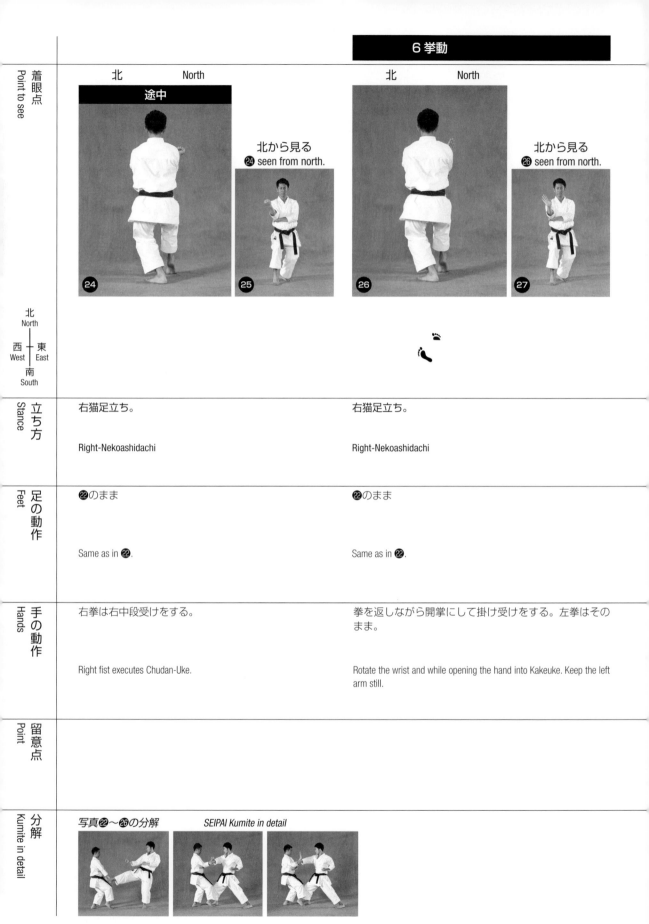

南　　　South	北西　　　Northwest	北西　　　Northwest

右三戦立ち。

Right-Sanchindachi.

右足を軸に体を180°回転、南方向に右三戦立ちとなる。

Pivoting on right foot, turn body 180 degree toward south then, Sanchindachi with right foot in front.

右開掌は握りながら左斜め下に締め込む。左拳は顔の前辺より半円を描くように下に回し、胸の前で右拳と交差したのち、左脇にしめる（相手の右肘関節を極める）。

While moving left fist up, then bringing it, downward in semi-circular motion, clench right hand. Then shoving downward diagonally to the left side. Crossing with right fist in front of chest, stopping under left side body (joint of opponent's right elbow is captured).

左手首が体の前に出ないよう脇をしめる。

Squeeze left side body with keeping left wrist does not come in front of body.

写真㉘〜㉜の分解　　SEIPAI Kumite in detail

7 挙動

	北西　　Northwest	北西　　Northwest

途中

北西から見る
㉜ seen from northwest.

北西から見る
㉞ seen from northwest.

北
North
西┼東
West｜East
南
South

立ち方 Stance	右三戦立ち。 Right-Sanchindachi.	左三戦立ち。 Left-Sanchindachi.
足の動作 Feet	左足を軸に体を北西方向（225°）に回転させ、右足を寄せて右三戦立ちとなる。 Pivoting on left foot, turn body 225 degree toward northwest, then, into Right-Sanchindachi.	左足より寄り足にて北西へ前進して左三戦立ちとなる。 Slide forward holding left Sanchindachi (left foot at first).
手の動作 Hands	左拳は開掌にして顔面前より円を描きながら掌を上前方にして左脇に構える。右拳は開掌にして腕を下に伸ばし、右掌にて下より上にはねあげる（弾指打ち）。 Left fist to Kaisho, after drawing a circle in front of the face, hold it under left armpit, with palm facing up forward. Right fist to Kaisho, extend arm downward, then, snap upward with right palm (attack with fingers).	左開掌を右肩前より回して掌底にて下段払い受け。右掌底は右下より押し上げる（支え上げ受け）。 Left-Shotei sweeps down from in front of right shoulder into Gedan-Haraiuke. Right-Shotei pushes up from the right into the opponent's left shoulder (Sasaeageuke).
留意点 Point	弾指打ち、手首のスナップを効かすようにする。 Attack with fingers. Use right wrist snap effectively.	
分解 Kumite in detail		

36　セーパイ　SEIPAI

8 挙動

北西（体は南西） Northwest (body faces southwest)	北西→南西 Northwest → Southwest	南西 Southwest

㊱ ㊲ ㊳

四股立ち。 Shikodachi		四股立ち。 Deep Shikodachi.
右足を北西方向に進め、四股立ちとなる。 Step right foot forward to northwest into Shikodachi.	右足で足払いをする。 Ashibarai with right foot.	右足払いから足幅はやや狭く、深い四股立ちとなる。 Making the stance slightly narrower, stamp down into a deep Shikodachi.
両掌を向かい合わせて水月部前に構える（左手下、右手上）。天地の構え。 Facing both palms each other, hold them in front of solar plexus (right hand above, left hand below). Tenchi-no-Kamae.	両掌を握りながら引きつける。両拳は乳の辺り。 Clenching both fists pull back until fists are about chest height.	両縦拳で下突き。 Punch downwards with both fists in Tateken.
	上体を上げずに足払いをすること。 Be sure to execute the sweep without lifting the upper body.	下突きで気合を入れる。 Perform with shout of Kiai "Ei!".

写真㉞〜㊳の分解　　*SEIPAI Kumite in detail*

		9 挙動	

北西（体は北東）Northwest (body faces northeast)　　　　北東　　　Northeast

途中

北東から見る
⓸ seen from northeast.

北
North

西—東
West | East

南
South

着眼点 Point to see

立ち方 Stance

四股立ち。

Shikodachi

右三戦立ち。

Right-Sanchindachi.

足の動作 Feet

左足を軸に右足を南東（180°）方向に引き、四股立ちとなる。

Pivoting on left foot, swing right foot 180 degree toward southeast.

右足より寄り足にて北東へ前進して右三戦立ちとなる。

Starting with the right foot, slide forward towards Northeast into right Sanchindachi.

手の動作 Hands

左払い受け。右拳は右脇に構える。

Left-Haraiuke. Hold right fist under right armpit.

右開掌を左肩前より回して掌底にて下段払い受け。左掌底は左下より押し上げる（支え上げ受け）。

Right-Shotei sweeps down from in front of left shoulder into Gedan-Haraiuke. Left-Shotei pushes up from the left into the opponent's right shoulder (Sasaeageuke).

留意点 Point

分解 Kumite in detail

38　セーパイ　SEIPAI

10 挙動

北東（体は南東） Northeast (body faces southeast)	北東→南東　Northeast → Southeast	南東　Southeast
 ㊷ 途中	 ㊸ 途中	 ㊹

四股立ち。 Shikodachi		四股立ち。 Deep Shikodachi.
左足を北東方向に進め、四股立ちとなる。 Step left foot forward to northeast.	左足で足払いをする。 Ashibarai with left foot.	左足払いから足幅はやや狭く、深い四股立ちとなる。 Making the stance slightly narrower, stamp down into a deep Shikodachi after left Ashi Barai.
両掌を向かい合わせて水月部前に構える（左手上、右手下）。天地の構え。 Facing both palms each other, hold them in front of solar plexus (left hand above, right hand below). Tenchi-no-Kamae.	両掌を握りながら引きつける。両拳は乳の辺り。 Clenching both fists pull back until fists are about chest height.	両縦拳で下突き。 Punch downwards with both fists in Tateken.
	上体を上げずに足払いをすること。 Be sure to execute the sweep without lifting the upper body.	下突きで気合を入れる。 Perform with shout of Kiai "Ei!".

39

		11 挙動		12 挙動
着眼点 Point to see		北東 （体は北西）Northeast (body faces northwest)	途中	南　　　South
立ち方 Stance		四股立ち。 Shikodachi		左猫足立ち。 Left-Nekoashidachi
足の動作 Feet		右足を軸に左足を南西（180°）方向に引き、四股立ちとなる。 Pivoting on right foot, swing left foot 180 degree toward southwest.	右足を左足の北方向に踏み出す。 With the right foot, step to the north of left foot.	体を南方向（135°）に回転させ、半身となり左足を引きつけ、左猫足立ちとなる。 Turn body 135 degree toward South into Hanmi, pull back left foot into Left-Nekoashidachi.
手の動作 Hands		右払い受け。左拳は左脇に構える。 Right-Haraiuke. Hold left fist under left armpit.		左中段受け。右拳は上段振り打ちをする（右拳は額の前で止める）。 Left-Chudan-Uke. Execute Jodan Furiuchi with right fist (stop right fist in front of the forehead).
留意点 Point				体の向きは半身になる。 The body is should be in 'Hanmi', facing diagonally.
分解 Kumite in detail			写真47の分解　　SEIPAI Kumite in detail	

40 セーパイ　SEIPAI

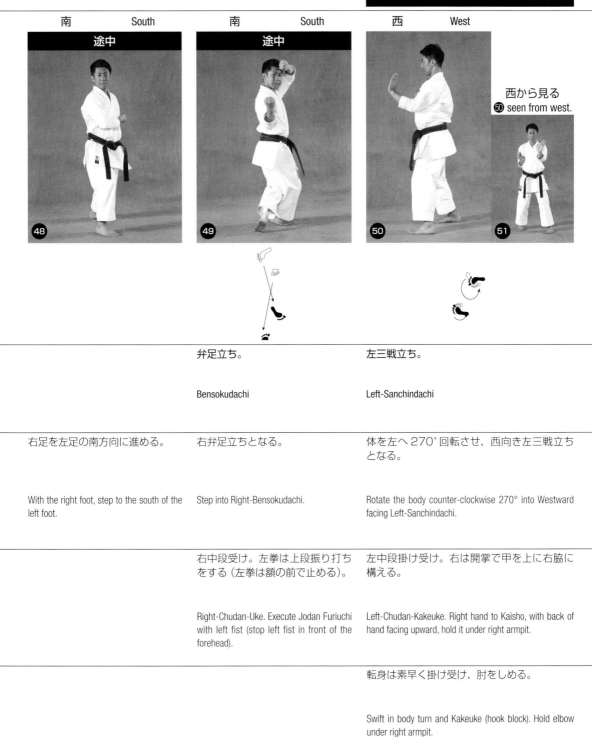

南 South	南 South	西 West
	弁足立ち。	左三戦立ち。
	Bensokudachi	Left-Sanchindachi
右足を左足の南方向に進める。	右弁足立ちとなる。	体を左へ270°回転させ、西向き左三戦立ちとなる。
With the right foot, step to the south of the left foot.	Step into Right-Bensokudachi.	Rotate the body counter-clockwise 270° into Westward facing Left-Sanchindachi.
	右中段受け。左拳は上段振り打ちをする（左拳は額の前で止める）。	左中段掛け受け。右は開掌で甲を上に右脇に構える。
	Right-Chudan-Uke. Execute Jodan Furiuchi with left fist (stop left fist in front of the forehead).	Left-Chudan-Kakeuke. Right hand to Kaisho, with back of hand facing upward, hold it under right armpit.
		転身は素早く掛け受け、肘をしめる。
		Swift in body turn and Kakeuke (hook block). Hold elbow under right armpit.

着眼点 Point to see	西（体は北）　West (body faces north) 途中 ⑫ 北から見る ❺❷ seen from north. ❺❸	西（体は北）　West (body faces north) 途中  北から見る ❺❹ seen from north. ❺❺

北 North / 西 West / 東 East / 南 South

立ち方 Stance	半後屈立ち。 Half-Kokutsudachi	半後屈立ち。 Half-Kokutsudachi
足の動作 Feet	体をひねり半後屈立ちとなる。 Twist body to be Harf-Kokutsudachi (right foot in front).	❺❷のまま。 Same as in ❺❷.
手の動作 Hands	左半打拳にて下段打ち。右開掌は握りながら右脇に構える。両足の向きを変えるのと腰のひねり、右膝を曲げるのを一気にすることで切れのある方向転換が出来る。 Strike to the left with Gedan-Uchi with the fist half closed, ('Han-Daken'). Clench right hand and hold it at the right side of the body. Execute a clean change of direction through changing the direction of both feet, twisting the hips and bending the right knee all at once.	左上段裏拳打ち。体と右拳はそのまま。 Left-Jyodan-Uraken-Uchi. Body and right fist remain the same.
留意点 Point		下段打ちから連続して上段裏拳打ちをする。裏拳打ちは素早く引き戻す。 Execute Gedan-Uchi and Jodan-Uraken-Uchi in fluid combination. Snap the Uraken-Uchi back quickly.
分解 Kumite in detail	写真❺❶〜❺❽の分解　　SEIPAI Kumite in detail	

14 挙動		15 挙動
西　West	西　West	西（体は北）　West (body faces north)

左三戦立ち。	左片足立ち。	四股立ち。
Left-Sanchindachi	Stand on left leg.	Shikodachi
体を西の方向にねじり、左三戦立ちにもどる。	右中段前蹴り。	右足を東の方向に引き、四股立ちとなる。
Twist body toward west, returning to Left-Sanchindachi.	Right-Chudan-Maegeri	Pull down right foot toward east.
右中段横受け。左拳は左脇に構える。	手の構えは❺❻のまま。	左中段裏突き（逆拳）。右手は開掌、指先を上に水月の前に構える（押え受け）。
Right-Chudan-Yokouke. Hold left fist under left armpit.	Same as in ❺❻.	Left-Chudan-Uratsuki (Gyakuken). Right hand to Kaisho, with fingers pointing upward, hold it in front of solar plexus (Osaeuke).
		裏突き。床と平行、伸ばしすぎない。
		Uratsuki. Keep parallel with floor and do not push out too much.

43

		16 挙動		
着眼点 Point to see		東　　　　East	東（体は北）　East (body faces north) 途中	東（体は北）　East (body faces north) 途中
		60	61	62
	北 North 西＋東 West　East 南 South			
立ち方 Stance		右三戦立ち。 Right-Sanchindachi	半後屈立ち。 Half-Kokutsudachi (right foot in front).	半後屈立ち。 Half-Kokutsudachi
足の動作 Feet		右足を軸に体を右へ回転（90°）させ、東向き。右三戦立ち。 Pivoting on right foot, turn body 90 degree toward right, facing east.	体をひねり半後屈立ちとなる。 Twist body.	61のまま。 Same as in 61.
手の動作 Hands		右中段掛け受け。左は開掌で左脇に構える。 Right-Chudan-Kakeuke. Hold left palm at the left side of the body.	右半打拳にて下段打ち。左開掌は握りながら左脇に構える。 Gedan-Uchi with right Half-Daken. Clenching left hand Kaisho, Hold it under left armpit.	右上段裏拳打ち。体と左拳はそのまま。 Right-Jyodan-Uraken-Uchi. Body and left fist remain the same.
留意点 Point				裏拳打ちは素早く引き戻す。 Snap the Uraken-Uchi back quickly.
分解 Kumite in detail				

44　セーパイ　SEIPAI

17 挙動		18 挙動
東　　　East	東　　　East	東（体は北）　East (body faces north)
	途中	
右三戦立ち。	右片足立ち。	四股立ち。
Right-Sanchindachi	Stand on right leg.	Shikodachi
体を東の方向にねじり、右三戦立ちにもどる。	左中段前蹴り。	左足を西の方向に引き、四股立ちとなる。
Twist body toward east, returning to Sanchindachi.	Left-Chudan-Maegeri	Pull down left foot toward west to stand Shikodachi.
左中段横受け。右拳は右脇に構える。	手の構えは❻❸のまま。	右中段裏突き（逆拳）。左手は開掌、指先を上に水月の前に構える（押え受け）。
Left-Chudan-Yokouke. Hold right fist under right armpit.	Same as in ❻❸.	Right-Chudan-Uratsuki (Gyakuken). Left hand Kaisho, with fingers pointing upward, hold it in front of solar plexus (Osaeuke).

着眼点 / Point to see	南 South 途中 ⓺⓺	南 South 途中 ⓺⓻	南 South 途中 ⓺⓼
北 North / 西 West / 東 East / 南 South			
立ち方 / Stance	右猫足立ち。 Right-Nekoashidachi	左猫足立ち。 Left-Nekoashidachi	左猫足立ち。 Left-Nekoashidachi
足の動作 / Feet	左足を北方向に1歩進め、左足を軸に体を南方向に回転（180°）右足を寄せて右猫足立ちとなる。 Take left foot one step toward north. Pivoting on left foot, turn body 180 degree toward south. Pull right foot together.	右足を北方向に1歩引くと同時に左足を寄せて左猫足立ちとなる。 While pulling back right foot one step toward north slide left foot together to stand Nekoashidachi (left foot in front).	⓺⓻のまま。 Same as in ⓺⓻.
手の動作 / Hands	両手を開掌にして、掌を向かい合わせて水月の前に構える（右手上、左手下）。天地の構え。 Both hands Kaisho, facing palms each other, hold them in front of solar plexus (right hand above, left hand below). Tenchi-no-Kamae.	両掌は向かい合わせたまま握りながら、円を描くように顔面辺りより右拳下、左拳が上になるようにねじり引き落とす。 With palms facing each other, clench both fists and drawing a circle in front of face, twist while pushing downward so that right fist comes to the bottom and left fist on top.	
留意点 / Point	両手は前に突き出さない。 Do not thrust out both hands.	両手は前方に伸ばさない。 Do not stretch out both hands.	
分解 / Kumite in detail	写真⓺⓺〜⓺⓽の分解　SEIPAI Kumite in detail 		

46　セーパイ　SEIPAI

19挙動

南　South　　　　　南　South　　　　　南　South

左猫足立ち。　　　　　　　　　　　　　　　　　結び立ち。

Left-Nekoashidachi　　　　　　　　　　　　　　Musubidachi

⑰のまま。　　　　　　　　　　　　　　　　　　左足を右足に引きつけ、結び立ちとなる。

Same as in ⑰.　　　　　　　　　　　　　　　　Bringing back left foot to right foot, return to Musubidachi.

右拳槌、左開掌にして下段回し打ちをする。　　右手は握り左手は開掌にして右拳を上、左掌を下に重ねる。　　回すように下腹部前に重ねて構える（左手前、右手後ろ）。

With right hand Kentsui and left hand Kaisho, execute Gedan-Mawashiuchi.　　With the right fist closed and the left hand open, raise the hands with the right fist on top and the left hand underneath.　　Turn the hands inwards and hold them in front of the lower abdomen, with the left hand in front.

		20 挙動	止め（直立）	礼
着眼点 Point to see		南　　　South 	南　　　South 	南　　　South
立ち方 Stance		結び立ち。 Musubidachi	結び立ち。 Musubidachi	結び立ち。 Musubidachi
足の動作 Feet		㉛のまま。 Same as in ㉛.	㉛のまま。 Same as in ㉛.	㉛のまま。 Same as in ㉛.
手の動作 Hands		ゆっくり右拳を開く。 Open the right hand slowly.	両手は開いて大腿部両側に付けて伸ばす。 Open both hands and extend down the stretched arms.	
留意点 Point				礼をする。 Rei (Bow)
分解 Kumite in detail				

48　セーパイ　SEIPAI

直立

南　　　South

結び立ち。

Musubidachi

⓹のまま。

Same as in ⓹.

⓻のまま。

Same as in ⓹.

ジオン
JION

特徴

おだやかな動きの中に激しい気魂のこもった形である。転進、転回、寄り足などを体得するのに適している形である。

練習に際しては特にむずかしい技はないが、平安、鉄騎の中にある種々の立ち方、技を正確に使って緩急のリズム、方向転換の際の手脚同時の基礎的動きが大切であり基本技を大変重んじた形である。

JION is KATA of calm movement combined with vibrant power. It is an ideal KATA for mastering techniques that require changing direction, rotating, Yoriashi (moving from the front foot), and so forth. In practice, there are no especially difficult techniques in this KATA. However, a lot of emphasis is placed on the accurate use of basic techniques including stances (also found in HEIAN and TEKKI), techniques employing puick/slow rhythm, and techniques using simultaneous movement of hand and foot while changing direction.

※従来の外受けを内受けに、内受けを外受けに統一した。
※The names have been consolidated so that what was once known as Sotouke is now Uchiuke, and Uchiuke is now Sotouke.

		直立	礼	直立
着眼点 Point to see		南　　South	南　　South	南　　South
		 ①	 ②	 ③
立ち方 Stance		結び立ち。 Musubidachi	結び立ち。 Musubidachi	結び立ち。 Musubidachi
足の動作 Feet		結び立ち。 Musubidachi	❶のまま。 Same as in ❶.	❶のまま。 Same as in ❶.
手の動作 Hands		両手は開いて大腿部両側に付けて伸ばす。 Open both hands and stretch down both sides of thighs.		手はそのまま。 Same as in ❶.
留意点 Point			礼をする。 Rei (Bow)	
分解 Kumite in detail				

北 North
西 West ／ 東 East
南 South

52　ジオン　JION

	用意	1 挙動	
	南　　　South	南　　　South	南東　　Southeast
			途中 

閉足立ち。	右前屈立ち。
Heisokudachi	Right-Zenkutsudachi

結び立ちから閉足立ちとなる。	左足を北に引く。
Move from Musubidachi to Heisokudachi.	Pull back left foot toward north.

右拳を左拳で包み、下顎前に拳2つくらい離して構える。両肘の間隔は肩幅程度。	両拳を胸前で交差させて右中段外受け。同時に左下段受けを行う。
Wrapping right fist with left palm, hold hands in front of lower part of jaw about two fists distance away. Space between both elbows is about shoulder width.	After crossing both fists in front of the the chest, execute Right-Chudan-Sotouke. At the same time, execute Left-Gedanuke.

	1〜12挙動は前屈立ちに注意する。後脚の張りが悪く、足刀部が床面に密着しないことのないように。 Motion 1 - 12 In Zenkutsudachi position, edge of back foot must stick to the floor.	【備考】全体において前屈立ちに注意する。前足の指先の方向と後足の指先の方向は同じ方向。両足が床面に密着すること（特に後足の足刀部）。 <Note>Pay attention to the form of Zenkutsudachi as a whole. The toes of both the front and rear foot should face the same direction, and make sure that all of the foot is firmly planted on the floor (in particular the edge of the rear foot).

	2 挙動	3 挙動	4 挙動
着眼点 Point to see	南東　　Southeast 	南東　　Southeast 	南東　　Southeast
立ち方 Stance	左前屈立ち。 Left-Zenkutsudachi	左脚立ち。 Stand on left foot.	右前屈立ち。 Right -Zenkutsudachi
足の動作 Feet	左足を1歩南東にすり出す。 Slide left foot one step out toward southeast.	南東に右中段前蹴り。 Right-Chudan-Maegeri to southeast.	右足を南東におろす。 Put down right foot toward southeast.
手の動作 Hands	両拳を胸前で交差して（右手、手前）ゆっくりしぼりながら両拳中段掻分け受け（甲斜め上）。 After crossing both fists (right hand inside) slowly, spread and hold them at Chudan-Kakiwakeuke, with back of hands facing diagonally upward.	❼のまま。 Same as in ❼.	右中段順突き。左拳は左腰に引く。 Right-Chudan-Juntsuki. Pull back left fist to the left hip.
留意点 Point	2～3挙動は中段掻分けより前蹴りの時の拳の位置は、そのまま。 Motion 2 - 3 Fist position same at Maegeri as after Chudan-Kakiwake.	【備考】3～4挙動は連続して行う。 <Note>Motion 3 - 4 must be done continuously.	
分解 Kumite in detail			

54　ジオン　JION

5 挙動	6 挙動	
南東　Southeast	南東　Southeast	南西　Southwest 途中
 ❿	 ⓫	 ⓬
右前屈立ち。 Right-Zenkutsudachi	右前屈立ち。 Right-Zenkutsudachi	
❾のまま。 Same as in ❾.	❾のまま。 Same as in ❾.	
左中段逆突き。右拳は右腰に引く。 Left-Chudan-Gyakutsuki. Pull back right fist to the right hip.	連続して右中段順突き。左拳は左腰に引く。 Execute Right -Chudan-Juntsuki continuously. Pull back left fist to the left hip.	
	【備考】5～6挙動は連続して行う。 <Note>Motion 5 - 6 must be done continuously.	

55

	7 挙動	8 挙動	9 挙動
着眼点 Point to see	南西　Southwest	南西　Southwest	南西　Southwest
	⑬	⑭	⑮
立ち方 Stance	右前屈立ち。 Right-Zenkutsudachi	右脚立ち。 Stand on the right foot.	左前屈立ち。 Left-Zenkutsudachi
足の動作 Feet	右足を南西にすり出す。 Slide right foot out toward southwest.	南西に左中段前蹴り。 Left-Chudan-Maegeri toward southwest.	左足を南西におろす。 Put down left foot toward southwest.
手の動作 Hands	両拳を胸前で交差して（右手、手前）ゆっくりしぼりながら両拳中段掻分け受け（甲斜め上）。 After crossing both fists (right hand inside) in front of the chest, execute Chudan-Kakiwakeuke while twisting both fists slowly (back of fists facing diagonally upwards).	⑬のまま。 Same as in ⑬.	左中段順突き。右拳は右腰に引く。 Left-Chudan-Junsuki. Pull back right fist to the right hip.
留意点 Point	7～8挙動は中段掻分けより前蹴りの時の拳の位置は、そのまま。 Motion 7 - 8 Fist position same at Maegeri as after Chudan-Kakiwake.	【備考】8～9挙動は連続して行う。 <Note>Motion 8 - 9 must be done continuously.	
分解 Kumite in detail			

56　ジオン　JION

10 挙動	11 挙動	
南西　Southwest	南西　Southwest	南　South

途中

左前屈立ち。	左前屈立ち。	
Left-Zenkutsudachi	Left-Zenkutsudachi	
⓯のまま。	⓯のまま。	
Same as in ⓯.	Same as in ⓯.	
右中段逆突き。左拳は左腰に引く。	連続して左中段順突き。右拳は右腰に引く。	
Right-Chudan-Gyakutsuki. Pull back left fist to the left hip.	Execute Left-Chudan-Juntsuki continuously. Pull back right fist to the right hip.	
	【備考】10～11挙動は連続して行う。	
	<Note>Motion 10 - 11 must be done continuously.	

		12挙動	13挙動	

		南　　　South	南　　　South	南　　　South

着眼点
Point to see

途中

⑲　⑳　㉑

北 North / 西 West ― 東 East / 南 South

立ち方 Stance		
左前屈立ち（半身）。 Left-Zenkutsudachi (Hips in Hanmi position).	左前屈立ち。 Left-Zenkutsudachi	

足の動作 Feet		
左足を南に移動させる（⑱は途中の姿勢止まらない）。 Move left foot forward south (⑱ Shows form during the move. Do not stop at this point).	⑲のまま。 Same as in ⑲.	

手の動作 Hands		
右掌をいったん額前に上げ、左拳は左腰から左前屈立ちと同時に左上段揚受け。右拳は右腰に引く。 As soon as the right hand is raised to the forehead, quickly execute Left-Jodan-Ageuke while simultaneously moving into Left-Zenkutsudachi. Pull the right fist to the hip.	右中段逆突き。左拳は左腰に引く。 Right-Chudan-Gyakutsuki. Pull back left fist to the left hip.	

留意点 Point		
	上段揚受けの時半身の姿勢をとる。腰の回転を充分にして12～13挙動は連続して行なう。 At Jyodan-Ageuke, body angle is about 45degree. Motion 12 - 13 must be done continuously.	

分解 Kumite in detail		

58　ジオン　JION

14 挙動	15 挙動	
南　　　South	南　　　South	南　　　South 途中
 ㉒	 ㉓	 ㉔

右前屈立ち（半身）。	右前屈立ち。	
Right-Zenkutsudachi (Hips in Hanmi position).	Right-Zenkutsudachi	
右足を南に進める。	㉒のまま。	
Step right foot toward south.	Same as in ㉒.	
左掌をいったん額前に上げ、右拳は右腰から右前屈立ちと同時に、右上段揚け。左拳は左腰に引く。	左中段逆突き。右拳は右腰に引く。	
As soon as the left hand is raised to the forehead, quickly execute Right-Jodan-Ageuke while simultaneously moving into Right-Zenkutsudachi. Pull the left fist to the hip.	Left-Chudan-Gyakutsuki. Pull back right fist to right hip.	
【備考】 14～15挙動は連続して行なう（㉑は途中の姿勢止まらない）。 <Note>Motion 14 - 15 must be done continuously (㉑ Shows form during the move. Do not stop at this point).		

	16 挙動	17 挙動	
	南　South	南　South	西　West

			途中
着眼点 Point to see	㉕	㉖	㉗

北 North / 西 West — 東 East / 南 South

	16挙動	17挙動	
立ち方 Stance	左前屈立ち（半身）。 Left-Zenkutsudachi (Hips in Hanmi position).	右前屈立ち。 Right-Zenkutsudachi	
足の動作 Feet	左足を南に進める。 Step left foot toward south.	右足を南に進める。 Step right foot toward south.	
手の動作 Hands	右掌をいったん額前に上げ、左拳は左腰から、左前屈立ちと同時に左上段揚げ受け。右拳は右腰に引く（㉔は途中の姿勢止まらない）。 As soon as the right hand is raised to the forehead, quickly execute Left-Jodan-Ageuke. while simultaneously moving into Left-Zenkutsudachi. Pull the right fist to the hip. The movement through ㉔ should flow, don't stop until ㉕.	右中段順突き。左拳は左腰に引く。 Right-Chudan-Juntsuki. Pull back left fist to the left hip.	両拳開掌。両腕をいったん胸前で交差する。 Both hands are open and flat, and should be immediately crossed in front of the chest.
留意点 Point		気合。 Kiai.	
分解 Kumite in detail			

60　ジオン　JION

18 挙動	19 挙動
西 West	西 West

北から見る
㉘ seen from north.

北から見る
㉚ seen from north.

右後屈立ち。	騎馬立ち。
Right-Kokutsudachi	Kibadachi
右脚を軸に体を左に回転させ左足を西に移す。	左足を西に進め、右足を引きつける（寄り足）。
Pivoting right foot turn the body to left and bring left foot to west.	Step left foot toward west and drag the right foot (Yoriashi).
両腕を互いに引っ張り合うようにして、右拳右側面上段受け、左拳左側面下段受け。	右鉤突き。左拳は左腰に引く。
Moving at the same time, right hand executes Sokumen-Jodan-Uke, while left hand executes Sokumen-Gedan-Uke.	Right-Kagitsuki. Pull back the left fist to the left hip.
後屈立ちで重心が前足にかかり過ぎない。重心の割合は後足 7、前足 3、のバランス。	【備考】右拳腰より。
At Kokutsudachi, don't put too much weight on the front foot. The balance of gravity should be 70% on the back foot and 30% on the front foot.	<Note>Right fist comes out from waist position.

20 挙動

着眼点 Point to see	東　　　East 途中 ㉜ 北から見る ㉜ seen from north. ㉝	東　　　East ㉞ 北から見る ㉞ seen from north. ㉟
	北 North 西╋東 West　East 南 South	
立ち方 Stance		左後屈立ち。 Left-Kokutsudachi
足の動作 Feet		東に向く。 Face east.
手の動作 Hands	両拳開掌。両腕をいったん胸前で交差する。 Both hands are open and flat, and should be immediately crossed in front of the chest.	両腕を互いに引っ張り合うようにして、左拳左側面上段受け、右拳右側面下段受け。㉘と反対姿勢（㉜は途中の姿勢止まらない）。 Moving at the same time, left hand executes Sokumen-Jodan-Uke, while right hand executes Sokumen-Gedan-Uke. This is a mirror of ㉘. ㉜ shows the position of the hands mid-movement; do not stop at this point.
留意点 Point		騎馬立ちから後屈立ちへ、後屈立ちから騎馬立ちへの変化があるが重心の移動が重要。 In changing from Kibadachi to Kokutsudachi and Kokutsudachi to Kibadachi, movement of the centre of gravity is most important.
分解 Kumite in detail		

62　ジオン　JION

21 挙動	22 挙動
東　East　　　北　North	北　North

騎馬立ち。	左前屈立ち（半身）。
Kibadachi	Left-Zenkutsudachi (Hips in Hanmi position).
右足を東に進め、左足を引きつける（寄り足）。	左足を北に進める（㊲は途中の姿勢止まらない）。
Step right foot toward east and drag the left foot (Yoriashi).	Step left foot toward north (㊲ Shows form during the move. Do not stop at this point).
左鉤突き。右拳は右腰に引く。	左下段払い。右拳は右腰に引く。
Left-Kagitsuki. Pull back right fist to the right hip.	Left-Gedanbarai. Pull back right fist to the right hip.
【備考】左拳腰より。	
<Note>Left fist comes out from the waist position.	

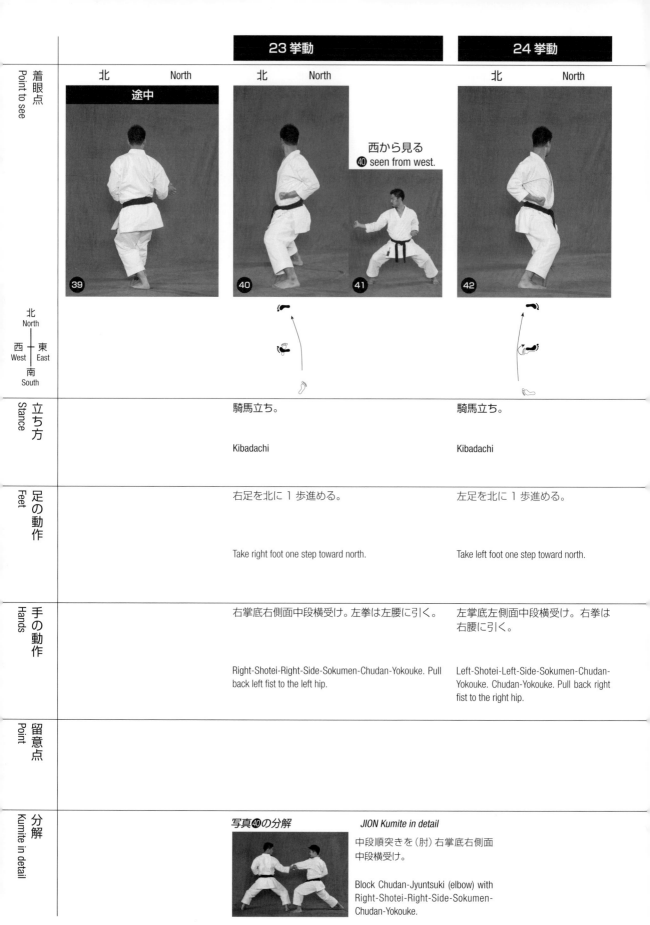

25 挙動		26 挙動
北 North	東 East	東 East

騎馬立ち。		右後屈立ち。
Kibadachi		Right-Kokutsudachi
右足を北に1歩進める。		右脚を軸に体を左に回転させ左足を東に移す。
Move right foot one step toward north.		Pivoting on right foot turn the body to the left and bring left foot toward east.
右掌底右側面中段横受け。左拳は左腰に引く。	両拳開掌。両腕をいったん胸前で交差する。	両腕を互いに引っ張り合うようにして、右拳右側面上段受け、左拳左側面下段受け。㉘と同じ（㊹は途中の姿勢止まらない）。
Right-Shotei-Right-Side-Sokumen-Chudan-Yokouke. Pull back left fist to the left hip.	Both hands are open and flat, and should be immediately crossed in front of the chest.	Moving at the same time, right hand executes Sokumen-Jodan-Uke, while left hand executes Sokumen-Gedan-Uke. This is the same as ㉘. (㊹ shows the position of the hands mid-movement; do not stop at this point.)

27 挙動

	東　　East	東　　East	西　　West
	途中		途中
	46	47	48

着眼点 / Point to see

北 North
西 West ― 東 East
南 South

立ち方 Stance		閉足立ち。 Heisokudachi	
足の動作 Feet		左足に右足を引きつける。 Pull right foot to left foot.	
手の動作 Hands		左拳左側面上段諸手受け、右拳は左肘内側に添える（甲下向）。左肘は左肩の高さ（**46**は途中の姿勢止まらない）。 The Left arm blocks left-side Jodan-Morote-Uke, with the right fist aligned with the inside of the left elbow. The left elbow should be shoulder-height. (**46** shows the form mid-movement; do not stop at this point.)	両拳開掌。両腕をいったん胸前で交差する。 Both hands are open and flat, and should be immediately crossed in front of the chest.
留意点 Point			
分解 Kumite in detail			

66　ジオン　JION

28 挙動		29 挙動
西 West	西 West	西 West
	途中	

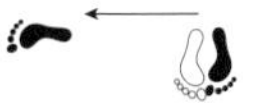

28 挙動	29 挙動
左後屈立ち。 Left-Kokutsudachi	閉足立ち。 Heisokudachi
右足を西に進める。 Step right foot toward west.	右足に左足を引きつける。 Pull left foot to the right foot.
両腕を互いに引っ張り合うようにして、左拳左側面上段受け。右拳右側面下段受け。㉞と同じ（㊽は途中の姿勢止まらない)。 Moving at the same time, left hand executes Sokumen-Jodan-Uke, while right hand executes Sokumen-Gedan-Uke. This is the same as ㉞ . (㊽ shows the position of the hands mid-movement; do not stop at this point.	右拳右側面上段諸手受け。左拳は右肘内側に添える（甲下向)。右肘は右肩の高さ（㊿は途中の姿勢止まらない)。 The right arm blocks right-side Jodan-Morote-Uke, with the left fist aligned with the inside of the right elbow. The right elbow should be shoulder-height. (㊿ shows the form mid-movement; do not stop at this point.)

写真㊾の分解 *JION Kumite in detail*

左下段蹴りを右下段受けで内側から受ける。左側面上段受け。

Block opponent's Left-Gedangeri with Right-Gedan-Uke from inside. Left-side-Jyodan-Uke.

		30 挙動		

		南　　　　South	南　　　　South	南　　　　South
着眼点 Point to see		途中 52	53	途中 54
	北 North 西—東 West East 南 South			
立ち方 Stance		閉足立ち。 Heisokudachi		
足の動作 Feet		⑤のまま。 Same as in ⑤.		
手の動作 Hands		両拳両側に掻分け、おろしながら構える（㊾は途中の姿勢止まらない）。 Spread both fists down to the both sides of the body and hold them there (㊾ Shows form before and after the move. Do not stop at these points).		
留意点 Point				
分解 Kumite in detail				

68　ジオン　JION

	31 挙動	32 挙動	

南　　　South　　　　　　南　　　South　　　　　　南　　　South

右足前交差立ち。	右前屈立ち。
Right foot front Kosadachi	Right-Zenkutsudachi

右足を南に大きく踏み込み、左足を引きつける。	左足を北に引く。
Take right foot a long step toward south, then, pull left foot together.	Pull back left foot toward north.

両拳で下段交差受け（右手上）。（㊹は途中の姿勢止まらない）	両拳を両側の下段へ掻分ける。
With the right fist on top, Gedan-Kousauke. (㊹ shows the form mid-movement; do not stop at this point.)	Spread fists down to the both sides of the body.

交差立ちは、右足に左足を充分に引きつける。	
At Kosadachi, pull right foot to the left foot closely.	

 position of hands.

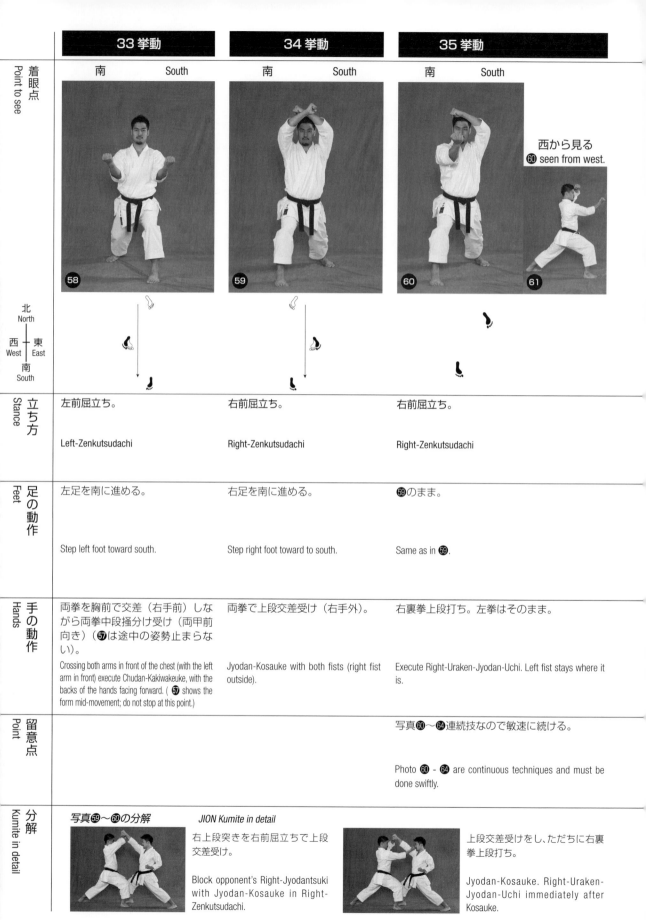

36 挙動	37 挙動
南 South	南 South

西から見る ❻❷ seen from west.　　西から見る ❻❹ seen from west.

右前屈立ち。	右前屈立ち。
Right-Zenkutsudachi	Right-Zenkutsudachi
❺❾のまま。	❺❾のまま。
Same as in ❺❾.	Same as in ❺❾.
左拳中段突受け、右背腕上段流し受け。	右裏拳上段打ち。同時に左腕は水月の前に添える。
Execute Left-Fist-Chudan-Tsukiuke with Right Haiwan-Jyodan-Nagashiuke.	While executing Right-Uraken-Jyodan-Uchi, hold left arm in front of solar plexus.

写真❻❷〜❻❹の分解　　JION Kumite in detail

すかさず左上段突きをするのを、右背腕上段流し受け。

When opponent attacks with Left-Jyodantsuki, immediately block with Right Haiwan-Jyodan-Nagashiuke.

ただちに右裏拳打ちをする。同時に左腕は左手甲を右肘に接し、水月前に添える。

Counter immediately with Right-Jyodan-Uraken-Uchi, while placing left arm in front of . Back of left hand touches right elbow.

		38 挙動	39 挙動
着眼点 Point to see		西　　　West	西　　　West
		途中 ⑥⑥	 ⑥⑦
			 ⑥⑧
	北 North 西 West ─ 東 East 南 South		
立ち方 Stance		左前屈立ち（半身）。 Left-Zenkutsudachi (Hips in Hanmi position).	右前屈立ち。 Right-Zenkutsudachi
足の動作 Feet		右脚軸に体を左に回転させて左足を西に移動させる。 Pivoting on the right foot turn the body to the left and bring left foot toward west.	右足を西に1歩進める。 Take right foot one step toward west.
手の動作 Hands		左中段外受け。右拳は右腰に引く（⑥⑥は途中の姿勢止まらない）。 Left-Chudan-Sotouke. Pull back right fist to the right hip (⑥⑥ Shows form during the move. Do not stop at this point).	右中段順突き。左拳は左腰に引く。 Right-Chudan-Juntsuki. Pull back left fist to the left hip.
留意点 Point			
分解 Kumite in detail			

72　ジオン　JION

	40 挙動	41 挙動
東　　　East	東　　　East	東　　　East

途中

69

70

71

	右前屈立ち（半身）。	左前屈立ち。
	Right-Zenkutsudachi (Hips in Hanmi position).	Left-Zenkutsudachi
	体を右に回転させ右足を東に進める。	左足を東に１歩進める。
	Turn the body to the right and step right foot forward to east.	Take left foot one step toward east.
	右中段外受け。左拳は左腰に引く（⑥⑨は途中の姿勢止まらない）。	左中段順突き。右拳は右腰に引く。
	Right-Chudan-Sotouke (⑥⑨ Shows form during the move. Do not stop at this point).	Left-Chudan-Juntsuki. Pull back right fist to the right hip.

体を右に回転させるとき、左足の
かかとを上げない。

When rotating the body to the right, make
sure not to raise the heel of the left foot.

73

42 挙動

	北　　　North	北　　　North	

途中

西から見る
73 seen from west.

北
North

西 ─┼─ 東
West │ East

南
South

着眼点 / Point to see

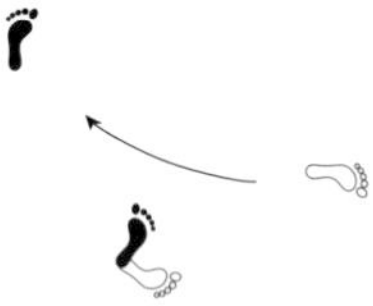

立ち方 / Stance

左前屈立ち（半身）。

Left-Zenkutsudachi (Hips in Hanmi position)

足の動作 / Feet

左足を北へ移す。

Bring left foot toward north.

手の動作 / Hands

左下段払い。右拳は右腰に引く。

Left-Gedanbarai. Right fist pulls back to the right hip.

留意点 / Point

分解 / Kumite in detail

74　ジオン　JION

43 挙動

北　North　　　北　North

75 西から見る
seen from west.

途中

騎馬立ち。

Kibadachi

右膝を高くあげて北へ踏み込む。

Lift right knee up high, then, step in toward north.

右拳は頭上高くふりあげ、右足を強く踏み込むと同時に、
右拳右側面中段打落し（⑦は途中の姿勢止まらない）。

Lift right fist over head, then stamp right foot in strongly while executing right side Chudan-Uchiotoshi with right fist (⑦ Shows form during the move. Do not stop at this point).

写真⑦～⑦の分解　　JION Kumite in detail

相手の中段順突きを右中段打落
しで叩き落とす。

Hip down opponent's Right-Chudantsuki with Right-Chudan-Uchiotoshi.

	44 挙動		45 挙動

着眼点 Point to see	北　　　North	北　　　North 途中	北　　　North
	78	79	80

北 North
西 West ─ 東 East
南 South

立ち方 Stance	騎馬立ち。 Kibadachi	騎馬立ち。 Kibadachi
足の動作 Feet	左膝を高くあげて北へ踏み込む。 Lift left knee up high, then, step in toward north.	右膝を高くあげて北へ踏み込む。 Lift right knee up to the height, then, step in toward north.
手の動作 Hands	左拳は頭上高くふりあげ、左足を強く踏み込むと同時に左拳左側面中段打落し。⑬と反対姿勢。右拳は右腰に引く（⑰は途中の姿勢止まらない）。 Lift right fist over head, then stamp left foot in strongly while executing Left-side-Chudan-Uchiotoshi with left fist. (Opposite posture of ⑬). Right fist pulls back to the right hip (⑰ Shows form during the move. Do not stop at this point).	右拳は頭上高くふりあげ、右足を強く踏み込むと同時に右拳右側面中段打落し。⑬と同じ。左拳は左腰に引く（⑲は途中の姿勢止まらない）。 Lift right fist over head, then stamp right foot in strongly while executing right side Chudan-Uchiotoshi with right fist. Same as in ⑬. Left fist pulls back to the left hip (⑲ Shows form during the move. Do not stop at this point).
留意点 Point		
分解 Kumite in detail		

76　ジオン　JION

46 挙動

東 East	東 East	西 West
途中		途中

	騎馬立ち。 Kibadachi	
	右脚軸に体を左に回転させ左足を引きつけながら東へ移動させる（寄り足ぎみ）。 Pivoting right foot turn the body to the left, then, slide left foot to east (drag) (Similar to Yoriashi).	
体を回転させながら右掌は左肩前、左拳（甲上向き）は右脇。 While turning body, the right palm comes in front of the shoulder, pull back left fist (back of hand faces upward) to the right side of the body.	両腕を交差し、互いに引きしぼる。右拳右乳前（甲上向き）左拳左側面中段突き（甲上向き）（❽は途中の姿勢止まらない）。 Cross both arms and squeeze them inside. Right fist comes in front of the right breast (back of hand faces upward) and execute Left-side Sokumen-Chudantsuki with left fist (❽ Shows form during the move. Do not stop at this point).	顔を西にむけると同時に左掌は右肩前、右拳（甲上向き）は左脇。 While facing west, left palm comes in front of the shoulder, pull back right fist (back of hand faces upward) to the side body.

写真❽～❽の分解　　JION Kumite in detail

相手の右中段順突きを右掌でつかみ、引き寄せながら、左拳左側面中段突き。

While taking hold of opponent's Right-Chudan-Juntsuki and drawing with right palm, execute Left-Sokumen-Chudantsuki with left fist.

	47 挙動	止め	直立
着眼点 Point to see	西 West	南 South	南 South
立ち方 Stance	騎馬立ち。 Kibadachi	閉足立ち。 Heisokudachi	結び立ち。 Musubidachi
足の動作 Feet	右足を西に移し、左足を引きつける（寄り足）。 Move right foot toward west, and, pull left foot drag (Yoriashi).	右足を左足に引きつける。 Pull right foot to the left foot.	結び立ち。 Musubidachi
手の動作 Hands	両腕を交差し、互いに引きしぼる。左拳は左乳前（甲上向き）、右拳は右側面中段突き（甲上向き）。 Cross both arms and squeeze them inside. Right fist comes in front of the left breast (back of hand faces upward) and right side Chudantsuki (back of hand faces upward) with right fist.	右拳を左拳で包み下顎前に構え、用意の姿勢にもどる。 Wrapping right fist with left palm, hold them in front of lower part of jaw, then return to Yo-i posture.	両手は開いて大腿部両側に付けて伸ばす。 Open both hands and stretch them along both thighs respectively.
留意点 Point	騎馬立ちで寄り足の時左右が流れないように。気合。 While standing Kibadachi position and in Yoriashi movement, left foot must not drift. kiai.	【備考】止めの時、残心に心がける。 <Note>At the position of Yame, a state of alertness is important.	
分解 Kumite in detail			

78　ジオン　JION

礼	直立
南　South	南　South

結び立ち。	結び立ち。
Musubidachi	Musubidachi
⑧のまま。	⑧のまま。
Same as in ⑧.	Same as in ⑧.
	⑧のまま。
	Same as in ⑧.
礼をする。	
Rei (Bow)	

カンクウダイ

KANKUDAI

特徴

　この形は四方、八方に敵を仮想して各方向からの様々な攻撃を捌き、受けて反撃するもので非常に変化に富んだ形である。技の緩急、力の強弱、体の伸縮はもちろん、転回、飛び上り、伏せなどがあり大変難しい形である。

KANKUDAI is a KATA requiring a variety of techniques in defense against opponents attacking from many directions and utilizes skillful counterattacks. It is an extremely difficult KATA using quick and slow techniques, strong and light power, and elastic body action suchas rotating, jumping, and dropping horizontally.

※従来の外受けを内受けに、内受けを外受けに統一した。
※The names have been consolidated so that what was once known as Sotouke is now Uchiuke, and Uchiuke is now Sotouke.

		直立	礼	直立
着眼点 Point to see		南　　South	南　　South	南　　South
		❶	❷	❸
			北 North 西 West ＋ 東 East 南 South	
立ち方 Stance		結び立ち。 Musubidachi	結び立ち。 Musubidachi	結び立ち。 Musubidachi
足の動作 Feet		結び立ち。 Musubidachi	❶のまま。 Same as in ❶.	❶のまま。 Same as in ❶.
手の動作 Hands		両手は開いて大腿部両側に付けて伸ばす。 Open both hands and stretch arms down to both sides of thighs.		手はそのまま。 Same as in ❶.
留意点 Point			礼をする。 Rei (Bow)	
分解 Kumite in detail				

82　カンクウダイ　KANKUDAI

		用意	1 挙動
	南　　South	南　　South	南　　South

	八字立ち。 Hachijidachi	八字立ち。 Hachijidachi	八字立ち。 Hachijidachi
	結び立ちから左足、右足の順に開いて八字立ち。 From Musubidachi, move the left foot, then right foot, out into Hachijidachi.	❹のまま。 Same as in ❹.	❹のまま。 Same as in ❹.
	両拳を大腿部前にもっていく。 Bring both fists to in front of the thighs.	静かにゆっくり両掌を右を上に斜めに重ねる。 Place both palms in front of the body with right palm on top.	両掌重ねたまま額斜め上に（❻は途中の姿勢止まらない）。 While placing right palm on left palm, lift them diagonally above forehead (❻ Shows form during the move. Do not stop at this point).
			【備考】ゆっくり。 指の間から空を観る気持ちで（目の高さより手の動きに合わせる）。 <Note>Do slowly. As if looking up to the sky between fingers (follow your hands upward when they reach eye level).

		2 挙動	3 挙動

着眼点 Point to see	南　　South 途中 ⑦	南　　South ⑧	東　　East ⑨
北 North 西 West ＋ 東 East 南 South			
立ち方 Stance	八字立ち。 Hachijidachi	八字立ち。 Hachijidachi	右後屈立ち。 Right-Kokutsudachi
足の動作 Feet	❹のまま。 Same as in ❹ .	❹のまま。 Same as in ❹ .	八字立ち自然体より左足を東へすり出す。 Slide left foot toward east (from Hachijidachi).
手の動作 Hands	両掌を左右に速く開き、止めずにゆっくりと下腹部前へ、両肘は軽く伸ばし静かに孤を描く。 Spread both palms swiftly to each side, then, bring them down slowly without stopping to the front of lower abdomen. Stretch both elbows lightly and describe an arc slowly.	左掌を縦に（甲斜め左下向き）右掌は左掌の上に斜めに軽く重ねる（右甲下向き）（❼は途中の姿勢止まらない）。 Left palm is vertical, (with back of hand facing diagonally downward to the left). Right hand is placed lightly on left palm (back of hand facing downward to the right) (❼ Shows form during the move. Do not stop at this point).	左背腕左側面上段受け（左甲北向き）。右掌胸前に構える（右甲下向き）。 Left-Haiwan-Left side Jyodan-Uke (Back of left hand faces north) Hold open right hand in front of chest (Back of right hand faces downward).
留意点 Point	【備考】開くとき、とめない。 <Note>Do not interrupt the motion after opening the arms.		【備考】後屈立ち、重心の割合は後足７、前足３のバランス。 <Note> For Kokutsudachi, the body weight is distributed 70% on the back leg, 30% on the front leg.
分解 Kumite in detail			

84　　カンクウダイ　KANKUDAI

4 挙動	5 挙動
西　　West	南　　South　　　南　　South

左後屈立ち。	八字立ち。
Left-Kokutsudachi	Hachijidachi
方向を西へ変える。	左後屈立ちから右脚を軸にして八字立ちになり、膝を軽く伸ばす。
Turn and face west.	Keeping the weight on the right leg pull the left leg in, extending the legs to slightly standing position.
右背腕右側面上段受け（右甲北向き）、左掌胸前に構える（左甲下向き）。	左中段縦手刀受け。右拳右腰に引く（左掌は右肘下からゆっくり大きく）（⓫は途中の姿勢止まらない）。
Right-Haiwan right side Jyodan-Uke. (Back of right hand faces north) Hold left palm in front of chest (Back of left hand faces downward).	Left-Chudan-Tate-Shutouke. Pull down right fist to right hip (make a slow large movement of the open left hand from under neath the right elbow) (⓫ Shows form during the move. Do not stop at this point).
❾～❿はサッと早く続ける（腕の動きより後屈立ちに注意）。	【備考】ゆっくり。
Motion ❾ - ❿ must be done quickly. Pay attention more to Kokutsudachi than arm movement.	<Note>Do slowly.

		6 挙動	7 挙動	8 挙動
着眼点 Point to see		南　　South ⑬	南　　South ⑭	南　　South ⑮
立ち方 Stance		八字立ち。 Hachijidachi	左膝屈。 Left-Hizakutsu	八字立ち。 Hachijidachi
足の動作 Feet		⑫のまま。 Same as in ⑫.	八字立ち自然体より足の位置そのまま腰左転。 Twist hips to the left without changing location of feet.	左膝屈を八字立ち自然体へもどす。 Return to Hachijidachi from Left-Hizakutsu.
手の動作 Hands		右中段突き。左拳左腰に引く。 Right-Chudantsuki. Pull back left fist to the left hip.	右中段外受け。左拳そのまま。 Right-Chudan-Sotouke. Left fist same as in ⑬.	左中段突き。右拳右腰に引く。 Left-Chudantsuki. Pull back right fist to the right hip.
留意点 Point			【備考】膝屈を正確に。両足が床面に密着すること（特に後足刀部）。 <Note>Do Hizakutsu accurately. Both foot must stick to the floor firmly (especially back foot edge).	
分解 Kumite in detail				

86　カンクウダイ　KANKUDAI

9 挙動	10 挙動
南　　　South	北　　　North

⑰ 北から見る
seen from north.

右膝屈。	左脚立ち。
Right-Hizakutsu	Standing on left foot.
八字立ち自然体より足の位置そのまま腰右転。	右膝屈より左足を半歩引き寄せ、左脚を軸として腰右転。右足裏を左膝横に添える。
Twist hips to right without changing location of feet.	Pull left foot half step forward from Right-Hizakutsu and stand on the left foot, then, pivoting on left foot, turn hips to the right. Place right foot sole lightly on the left knee.
左中段外受け。右拳⑮のまま。	両拳左腰構え。右拳（甲前向）を左拳の上（甲下向）に重ねる。
Left-Chudan-Sotouke. Right fist same as in ⑮.	Hold both fists on the left hip, with right fist (back of fist facing outside) on top of the left fist (back of fist facing downward).
【備考】⑭と同じく。	両拳をしっかりと左腰に引く。
<Note>Same as in ⑭.	Firmly pull both fists back to the left hip.

		11 挙動		12 挙動	13 挙動
着眼点 Point to see		北　　North		南　　South	南　　South
		⑲⑳ 北から見る ⑲ seen from north.		㉑	㉒
立ち方 Stance		左脚立ち。 Standing on the left foot.		右後屈立ち。 Right-Kokutsudachi	左後屈立ち。 Left-Kokutsudachi
足の動作 Feet		北へ右横蹴上げ。 Right-Yokokeage toward north.		右足を北におろす。 Put down right foot toward north.	右足南へ 1 歩進める。 Take right foot one step toward south.
手の動作 Hands		右裏拳上段横回し打ち。左拳そのまま。 Jyodan-Yokomawashiuchi with Right-Uraken. Left fist same as in ⑰.		左手刀中段受け。右手刀胸前。 Left-Shuto-Chudan-Uke. Hold Right-Shuto in front of the chest.	右手刀中段受け。左手刀胸前。 Right-Shuto-Chudan-Uke. Hold Left-Shuto in front of the chest.
留意点 Point		【備考】蹴上げ（目標中段）。 <Note> Keage is Chudan.			
分解 Kumite in detail					

88　カンクウダイ　KANKUDAI

14 挙動	15 挙動	
南　　　South	南　　　South	途中

北から見る
㉖ seen from north.

右後屈立ち。	右前屈立ち。
Right-Kokutsudachi	Right-Zenkutsudachi
左足南へ１歩進める。	右足南へ１歩進める。
Take left foot one step toward south.	Take right foot one step toward south.
左手刀中段受け。右手刀胸前。	右中段四本貫手（甲右向き）。左掌中段押え受け（右肘下、甲上向き）。
Left-Shuto-Chudan-Uke. Hold Right-Shuto in front of the chest.	Right-Chudan-Shihon-Nukite (back of hand facing upward). Left-Palm-Chudan-Osaeuke (underneath left elbow, back of hand facing upward).

①気合い。
②前屈立ちを正確に。足刀及び足裏を床面に密着させる。
【備考】足刀及び足裏を床面に対する密着は全てに言える。
① Kiai
② Zenkutsudachi must be done accurately. Contact Sokuto (edge of foot) and Ashiura (sole of foot) with floor firmly.
<Note>This contacting the feet with the floor can be said to apply for every case.

		16 挙動	17 挙動
着眼点 Point to see		北 North 27 北から見る ㉗ seen from north. 28	北 North 29 北から見る ㉙ seen from north. 30
立ち方 Stance		左前屈立ち（逆半身）。 Left-Zenkutsudachi (hips in reverse Hanmi).	左脚立ち。 Stand on the left foot.
足の動作 Feet		右脚を軸に腰を左転し北へ向く。 Pivoting on right foot, turn hips to the left, facing north.	右前蹴り。 Right-Maegeri
手の動作 Hands		右手刀上段横回し打ち。左掌額前上段受け（㉕は途中の姿勢止まらない）。 Jyodan-Yokomawashiuchi with Right-Shuto. Left-palm-Jyodan-Uke in front of forehead (㉕ Shows form during the move. Do not stop at this point).	上体㉗のまま。 Same as in ㉗.
留意点 Point			
分解 Kumite in detail			

90　カンクウダイ　KANKUDAI

18挙動

南　　　South

途中 ｜ ㉜ 西から見る seen from west.

右後屈立ち。

Right-Kokutsudachi

右足を北におろす。

While putting down right foot toward north, turn hips to left.

右拳右側面上段受け。左拳左側面下段受け（いったん右掌を左肘下から、左掌は右肩口から握りながら互いに引きしぼるように）（㉛は途中の姿勢止まらない）。

Right fist Right side Jyodan-Uke. Left fist Left side Gedan-Uke (gripping both fists, pull apart right fist from underneath left elbow and left fist from top of right shoulder) ㉛ Shows form during the move. Do not stop at this point).

19挙動	20挙動

着眼点 / Point to see

南　South | 南　South

北から見る
❸❺ seen from north.

㉞ | ㉟ | ㊱

北 North
西 West ｜ 東 East
南 South

立ち方 / Stance	左前屈立ち。	左足前レの字立ち。
	Left-Zenkutsudachi	Stand naturally, with left foot in front.

足の動作 / Feet	右脚を軸に、左足を前屈立ちに膝を屈する。	左足を右足にすこし引き寄せる。
	Pivoting on the right foot, bend left knee to Zenkutsudachi.	Pull left foot to the right foot slightly.

手の動作 / Hands	右手刀下段打込み（甲下向き）。左掌上段流し受け（甲横向き）。	左拳下段に伸ばす。右拳右腰に引く。
	Right-Shuto-Gedan-Uchikomi (back of hand facing downward). Left-palm-Jyodan-Nagashiuke above the right shoulder (back of hand facing outside).	Stretch left fist downward. Pull back right fist to right hip.

留意点 / Point		【備考】ゆっくり。
		<Note>Do slowly.

分解 / Kumite in detail		

92　カンクウダイ　KANKUDAI

21 挙動	22 挙動	
南　　　South	南　　　South	

左前屈立ち（逆半身）。	左脚立ち。
Left-Zenkutsudachi (hips in reverse Hanmi).	Stand on the left foot.
右足そのままの位置で腰を左転。左足を進め、前屈立ちとなる。	右前蹴り。
Turn hips to left without changing location of right foot.	Right-Maegeri
右手刀上段横回し打ち。左掌額前上段受け。	上体❸のまま。
Jyodan-Yokomawashiuchi with Right-Shuto. Left-palm-Jyodan-Uke in front of forehead.	Same as in ❸ .

	23 挙動	24 挙動
着眼点 Point to see	北　North ㊶ 北から見る ㊶ seen from north. ㊷	北　North ㊸ 北から見る ㊸ seen from north. ㊹
立ち方 Stance	右後屈立ち。 Right-Kokutsudachi	左前屈立ち。 Left-Zenkutsudachi
足の動作 Feet	右足を南におろす。 Put down right foot toward south.	右脚を軸に左脚を前屈立ちに膝を屈する。 Pivoting on the right foot, bend left knee to Zenkutsudachi.
手の動作 Hands	右拳右側面上段受け。左拳左側面下段受け（要領は㉜と同様）。 Right-fist-right-side-Jyodan-Uke. Left-fist-left-side-Gedan-Uke (Movement same as in ㉜).	右手刀下段打込み（甲下向き）。左掌上段流し受け（甲横向き）。 Right-Shuto-Gedan-Uchikomi (back of hand facing downward). Left-palm-Jyodan-Nagashiuke above right shoulder (back of hand facing outside).
留意点 Point		
分解 Kumite in detail		

25 挙動	26 挙動
北　　　North	西　　　West

北から見る
㊻ seen from north.

左足前レの字立ち。	右脚立ち。
Stand naturally with left foot in front.	Stand on right foot.
左足を右足にすこし引き寄せる。	右脚を軸として腰を左転、左足裏を右膝横に添える。
Pull left foot to the right foot slightly.	Pivoting on the right foot, turn the hips to left. Place left sole on the right knee.
左拳下段に伸ばす。右拳右腰に引く。	両拳右腰構え。左拳（甲前向き）を右拳の上（甲下向き）に重ねる。
Stretch left fist downward. Pull back right fist to the right hip.	Hold both fists on the right hip with left fist (back of fist facing outside) on top of the right fist (back of fist facing downward).
ゆっくり。	
Do slowly.	

		27 挙動	28 挙動
着眼点 Point to see		西　　　　West 北から見る ❸ seen from north.	西　　　　West 北から見る ❺ seen from north.
		北 North 西┼東 West│East 南 South	
立ち方 Stance		右脚立ち。 Stand on right foot.	左前屈立ち。 Left-Zenkutsudachi
足の動作 Feet		西へ左横蹴上げ。 Left-Yokokeage toward west.	左脚を西へおろし、腰を左転し左前屈立ちとなる。 Put down left foot toward west and turn hips to the left to pose Left-Zenkutsudachi.
手の動作 Hands		左裏拳上段横回し打ち。右拳❹のまま。 Jyodan-Yokomawashiuchi with Left-Uraken. Right fist same as in ❹.	右前猿臂（左掌に当てる）。 Right-elbow-Enpi (hitting against the left palm).
留意点 Point		横蹴上げの場合、上体が力み過ぎて引手が横蹴上げと同時に離れないこと。 【備考】蹴上げ（目標中段）。 For Yokokeage, avoid tensing the upper body too much, and that the pulled hand doesn't come away from the body when kicking. <Note> Keage is Chudan.	【備考】左腕平行。 <Note>Left arm is parallel with floor.
分解 Kumite in detail			

96　カンクウダイ　KANKUDAI

29 挙動	30 挙動
東 East	東 East
  北から見る ㊺ seen from north.	  北から見る ㊺ seen from north.
左脚立ち。	左脚立ち。
Stand on left foot.	Stand on the left foot.
左脚を軸に腰を右転しながら右足裏を左膝横に添える。	東へ右横蹴上げ。
Pivoting on the left foot, turn hips to the right. Place right sole on left knee.	Right-Yokokeage toward east.
両拳左腰構え。右拳（甲前向き）を左拳の上（甲下向き）に重ねる。	右裏拳上段横回し打ち。左拳㊺のまま。
Hold both fists on the left hip with right fist (back of fist facing outside) on top of the left fist (back of fist facing downward).	Jyodan-Yokomawashiuchi with Right-Uraken. Left fist same as in ㊺.
	【備考】蹴上げ（目標中段）。
	<Note> Keage is Chudan.

	31 挙動	32 挙動
着眼点 Point to see	東　East	西　West
	56 57 北から見る 56 seen from north.	58 59 北から見る 58 seen from north.

北
North

西 — 東
West｜East
南
South

	31 挙動	32 挙動
立ち方 Stance	右前屈立ち。 Right-Zenkutsudachi	右後屈立ち。 Right-Kokutsudachi
足の動作 Feet	右足を東へおろし、腰を右転し右前屈立ちとなる。 Put down right foot toward east and turn hips to the right.	右脚を軸にし、腰を左転。 Pivoting on right foot, turn hips to the left.
手の動作 Hands	左前猿臂（右掌に当てる）。 Left-elbow-Empi (hitting against right palm).	左手刀中段受け。右手刀胸前。 Left-Shuto-Chudan-Uke. Hold Right-Shuto in front of the chest.
留意点 Point	【備考】右腕平行。 <Note>Right arm is parallel with floor.	
分解 Kumite in detail		

98　カンクウダイ　KANKUDAI

33 挙動	34 挙動
北西　Northwest	東　East
 　⑥⓪ seen from north.	 　⑥② seen from north.

左後屈立ち。	左後屈立ち。
Left-Kokutsudachi	Left-Kokutsudachi
左脚を軸に右足を北西に１歩進める。	左脚を軸に右足を東に１歩進める。
Pivoting on left foot, take right foot one step toward northwest.	Pivoting on left foot, take right foot one step toward east.
右手刀中段受け。左手刀胸前。	右手刀中段受け。左手刀胸前。
Right-Shuto-Chudan-Uke. Hold Left-Shuto in front of the chest.	Right-Shuto-Chudan-Uke. Hold Left-Shuto in front of the chest.

		35 挙動	36 挙動
着眼点 Point to see		北東　Northeast 64 北から見る 64 seen from north.	北　North 66 北から見る 66 seen from north.
北 North 西 West 東 East 南 South			
立ち方 Stance		右後屈立ち。 Right-Kokutsudachi	左前屈立ち（逆半身）。 Left-Zenkutsudachi
足の動作 Feet		右脚を軸に左足を北東に1歩進める。 Pivoting on right foot, take left foot a step toward northeast.	左足を北に移す。 Bring left foot to north.
手の動作 Hands		左手刀中段受け。右手刀胸前。 Left-Shuto-Chudan-Uke. Hold Right-Shuto in front of the chest.	右手刀上段横回し打ち。左掌額前上段受け。 Jyodan-Yokomawashiuchi (hips in reverse Hanmi) with Right-Shuto. Left-palm-Jyodan-Uke in front of forehead.
留意点 Point			
分解 Kumite in detail			

100　カンクウダイ　KANKUDAI

37 挙動

北 North  北 North

左脚立ち。

Stand on the left foot.

北へ右前蹴り。

Right-Maegeri toward north.

手の位置は❻のまま。

Hands position is same as in ❻.

蹴り足を戻しながら左掌を前に出し（甲上）、右拳を額前に持っていく。

When retracting the kick extend the left hand out in front (back of hand facing upwards), and bring the right fist to in front of the forehead.

	38 挙動	39 挙動
着眼点 Point to see	北　　North 72　　73 北から見る ❼❷ seen from north.	北　　North 74　　75 北から見る ❼❹ seen from north.
	北 North 西 West ┼ 東 East 南 South	
立ち方 Stance	右脚前交差立ち（左足を右足後ろに交差）。 Kosadachi with right foot in front (left foot comes behind right ankle).	右前屈立ち（半身）。 Right-Zenkutsudachi (hips in Hanmi position)
足の動作 Feet	右足から北へ大きく飛び込む。 Take a long jumping step toward north, with right foot at first.	左足を南へ引く。 Pull back left foot toward south.
手の動作 Hands	右裏拳縦回し打ち。左拳左腰に引く（❼❶は途中の姿勢止まらない）。 Right-Uraken-Tatemawashiuchi. Pull back left fist to the left hip (❼❶ Shows form during the move. Do not stop at this point).	右中段外受け。左拳左腰に引く。 Right-Chudan-Sotouke. Hold left fist on the left hip.
留意点 Point	交差立ちは右足に左足を充分に引きつける。 At Kosadachi position, draw right foot to left foot closely.	
分解 Kumite in detail		

102　カンクウダイ　KANKUDAI

40 挙動	41 挙動

北　　　North

北から見る
㊆ seen from north.

76　77

北　　　North

北から見る
㊆ seen from north.

78　79

右前屈立ち。	右前屈立ち。
Right-Zenkutsudachi	Right-Zenkutsudachi
㊆のまま。	㊆のまま。
Same as in ㊆.	Same as in ㊆.
左中段逆突き。右拳右腰に引く。	右中段順突き。左拳左腰に引く。
Left-Chudan-Gyakutsuki. Pull back right fist to the right hip.	Right-Chudan-Jyuntsuki. Pull back left fist to the left hip.
	【備考】㊆、㊆は連続で。
	<Note>㊆ and ㊆ must be done in continuous movement.

サイファ　セーパイ　ジオン　**カンクウダイ**　バッサイダイ　セイエンチン　セイシャン　チントウ

		42 挙動	43 挙動
着眼点 Point to see		南　　　South 途中 ⑧	南　　　South ⑧	南　　　South ⑧
	北 North 西 West ─ 東 East 南 South		
立ち方 Stance		左脚立ち。 Stand on the left foot	右足前伏せ（右前屈）。 Fuse with right foot in front. (Right-Zenkutsu)
足の動作 Feet		左脚を軸に腰左転、南へふり向き、右膝を高くかい込む。 Pivoting on the left foot, turn hips to the left, facing south, then, lift right knee up high.	左脚を軸に右足を南へおろし、右膝を充分に屈し、体を地に伏せる。 Put down right foot toward south. Bend right knee deeply, then, drop to the body Fuse style.
手の動作 Hands		右裏突き。左掌右手首横添え（両手を右大腿の両側からすり上げる）。 Right-Uratsuki. Scoop up hands from both sides of right thigh and place left palm on the right wrist.	両掌肘立伏せ。 Push up with both palms.
留意点 Point		両腕を右大腿の両側からすり上げる。このとき、右膝を高くかい込むこと。 Both hands glide up from both sides of right thigh. At this time right knee is lifted high.	後足の足刀部が床面より浮いてはならない。床面に密着すること。 【備考】4mぐらい前を見る。 Don't lift edge of back foot from floor. Foot edge must stick to the floor. <Note>Look at about 4m front.
分解 Kumite in detail	写真⑧〜⑧の分解　　KANKUDAI Kumite in detail 		左脚を軸として左転、後方へふり向くと同時に右膝を高くあげ、両掌は右腿左右両側からすり出すようにして右拳（甲下）手首に左掌を添えて突き出す。あげた右膝頭と右手肘は拳1つくらいの間隔をとる。 Pivoting on the left foot, turn to the left. When body turns 180 degrees, lift right knee up high, and scoop up hands from both sides of right thigh, with left palm placed on the wrist of right hand (back of hand facing downward), and thrust them forward. Leave space about one fist between lifted right kneecap and right elbow.

104　カンクウダイ　KANKUDAI

44 挙動	45 挙動
北 North	北 North

北から見る ❽ seen from north.　　　北から見る ❽ seen from north.

右後屈立ち。	左後屈立ち。
Right-Kokutsudachi	Left-Kokutsudachi
右脚を軸に腰左転、北へふり向く。	右足を北へ1歩進める。
Pivoting on the right foot, turn hips to the left, facing north.	Take right foot one step toward north.
左手刀下段受け（甲上向き）。右手刀胸前構え（甲下向き）。	右手刀中段受け。左手刀胸前。
Left-Shuto-Gedan-Uke (back of hand facing upward). Hold Right-Shuto (back of hand facing downward) in front of the chest.	Right-Shuto-Chudan-Uke. Hold Left-Shuto in front of the chest.

写真 ❽〜❽の分解　　KANKUDAI Kumite in detail

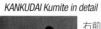

右前屈、両掌は軽く地に着けて伏せる姿勢。ただし顔は4mぐらい前方を見つめる気持ちでややあげる。

Right-Zenkutsu, both palms are touched to the floor lightly in Fuse position. In this case face is lifted up a little looking at about 4m front.

105

	46 挙動	47 挙動	48 挙動
着眼点 Point to see	東　　　East	東　　　East	西　　　West
	87	88	89
立ち方 Stance	左前屈立ち（半身）。 Left-Zenkutsudachi (hips in Hanmi position).	左前屈立ち。 Left-Zenkutsudachi	右前屈立ち（半身）。 Right-Zenkutsudachi (hips in Hanmi position).
足の動作 Feet	右脚を軸とし、腰を左転、左足を東に移動させる。 Pivoting on the right foot, turn hips to the left, bring left foot toward east.	87のまま。 Same as in 87.	左脚を軸に腰を右転、西を向く。 Pivoting on the left foot, turn hips to the right, facing west.
手の動作 Hands	左中段外受け。右拳右腰に引く。 Left-Chudan-Sotouke. Pull back right fist to the right hip.	右中段逆突き。左拳左腰に引く。 Right-Chudan-Gyakutsuki. Pull back left fist to the left hip.	右中段外受け。左拳右腰に引く。 Right-Chudan-Sotouke. Pull back left fist to the left hip.
留意点 Point			
分解 Kumite in detail			

106　カンクウダイ　KANKUDAI

49 挙動	50 挙動	51 挙動
西　West	西　West	北　North

右前屈立ち。

Right-Zenkutsudachi

89のまま。

Same as in 89.

左中段逆突き。右拳右腰に引く。

Left-Chudan-Gyakutsuki. Pull back right fist to the right hip.

右前屈立ち。

Right-Zenkutsudachi

89のまま。

Same as in 89.

右中段順突き。左拳左腰に引く。

Right-Chudan-Juntsuki. Pull back left fist to the left hip.

【備考】90 91は連続で。

<Note> 90 and 91 must be done in continuous movement.

左脚立ち。

Stand on left foot.

左脚を軸に右足裏を左膝横に添える。

Pivoting on the left foot lift right foot up to side of left knee.

両拳左腰構え左脚立ち。右拳（甲前向き）を左拳の上（甲下向き）に重ねる。

Hold both fists on the left hip with right fist (back of hand facing outside) on top of the left fist (back of hand facing downward).

92 北から見る
92 seen from north.

107

		52 挙動	53 挙動
着眼点 Point to see		北　North	南　South
		94 北から見る 94 seen from north. 95	96
立ち方 Stance		左脚立ち。 Stand on the left foot.	右後屈立ち。 Right-Kokutsudachi
足の動作 Feet		北へ右横蹴上げ。 Right-Yokokeage toward north.	右足を北におろす。 Put down right foot toward north.
手の動作 Hands		右裏拳上段横回し打ち。 Jyodan-Yokomawashiuchi with Right-Uraken.	左手刀中段受け。右手刀胸前。 Left-Shuto-Chudan-Uke. Hold Right-Shuto in front of the chest.
留意点 Point		【備考】蹴上げ（目標中段）。 <Note> Keage is Chudan.	
分解 Kumite in detail			

108　カンクウダイ　KANKUDAI

54 挙動

南　　　South

右前屈立ち。

Right-Zenkutsudachi

右足を南へ1歩進める。

Take right foot one step toward south.

右中段四本貫手（甲右向き）。左掌中段押え受け（右肘下、甲上向き）。

Right-Chudan-Shihon-Nukite (back of hand facing upward). Left-Palm-Chudan-Osaeuke (underneath left elbow, back of hand facing upward).

98から100までは途中止まらない。

Do not stop from 98 to 100.

	55 挙動	56 挙動	57 挙動
着眼点 Point to see	南　South 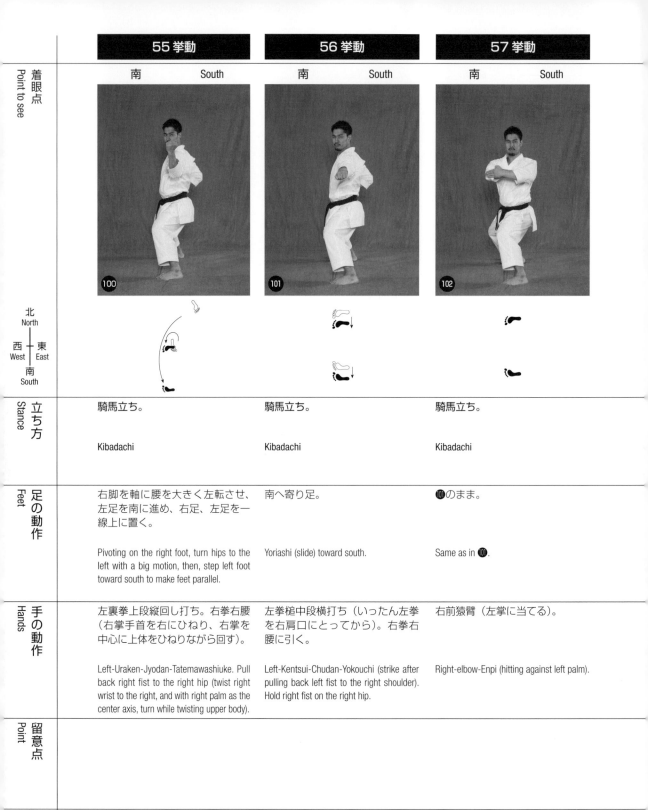	南　South	南　South
立ち方 Stance	騎馬立ち。 Kibadachi	騎馬立ち。 Kibadachi	騎馬立ち。 Kibadachi
足の動作 Feet	右脚を軸に腰を大きく左転させ、左足を南に進め、右足、左足を一線上に置く。 Pivoting on the right foot, turn hips to the left with a big motion, then, step left foot toward south to make feet parallel.	南へ寄り足。 Yoriashi (slide) toward south.	⑩のまま。 Same as in ⑩.
手の動作 Hands	左裏拳上段縦回し打ち。右拳右腰（右掌手首を右にひねり、右掌を中心に上体をひねりながら回す）。 Left-Uraken-Jyodan-Tatemawashiuke. Pull back right fist to the right hip (twist right wrist to the right, and with right palm as the center axis, turn while twisting upper body).	左拳槌中段横打ち（いったん左拳を右肩口にとってから）。右拳右腰に引く。 Left-Kentsui-Chudan-Yokouchi (strike after pulling back left fist to the right shoulder). Hold right fist on the right hip.	右前猿臂（左掌に当てる）。 Right-elbow-Enpi (hitting against left palm).
留意点 Point			

分解 Kumite in detail

写真⑰〜⑩の分解　　KANKUDAI Kumite in detail

右手を右回しに逆にひねられたとき、上体を前に出しながら右手を右肩の上に、体と共に肘を中心にひねり回しながら、右脚を軸にして左回りに左足を前方に移す。

When right hand is twisted to right by opponent, thrust upper body forward, with right hand on right shoulder, then, twist body with elbows and pivoting on right foot, swing left foot toward front.

110　カンクウダイ　KANKUDAI

58 挙動	59 挙動
北　　　　North	北　　　　North

北から見る
seen from north.

騎馬立ち。	騎馬立ち。
Kibadachi	Kibadachi
⑩のまま。	⑩のまま。
Same as in ⑩.	Same as in ⑩.
両拳左腰構え。右拳（甲前向き）を左拳の上（甲下向き）に重ねる。	右下段払い。左拳左腰に引く。
Hold both fists on the left hip with right fist (back of hand facing outside) on top of the left fist (back of hand facing downward).	Right-Gedanbarai. Hold left fist on the left hip.

60 挙動

着眼点 / Point to see	途中 / 北から見る (105 seen from north.) / 東 East / 北から見る (109 seen from north.) 106 107 108 109 北 North 西 West 東 East 南 South	
立ち方 / Stance		騎馬立ち。 Kibadachi
足の動作 / Feet		右脚を軸に腰を大きく右転、左足は膝を上げてすばやく北へ踏み込む。 Pivoting on the right foot, turn hips to right with a big motion, and lift left knee high, then, stamp down left foot toward north.
手の動作 / Hands		左拳下段受け（甲後向き）。右拳ふりあげ（甲後向き）左拳は大きく頭上から回しながら振りおろし、同時に右拳は頭上へ振りあげる（106は途中の姿勢止まらない）。 Left-Gedan-Uke (back of hand facing backward). Swing right fist above head (back of hand facing backward) while swinging down left fist from above head in a large arcline motion (106 Shows form during the move. Do not stop at this point).
留意点 / Point		左拳は小指側で下段受け。左足は敏速に行う。 Left-Gedan-Uke is executed at little finger side of the left fist. Left foot must move quickly.
分解 / Kumite in detail	写真109〜110の分解　KANKUDAI Kumite in detail  	相手の中段右前蹴りに対し、頭上より、すばやく足首を流すように下段受けし、縦拳（落し突き）にして突く（右拳甲外）。 Against Chudan-Right-Maegeri by opponent, Gedan-Uke by drifting down the ankle and thrust Tatekentsuki (Otoshitsuki) (back of right hand faces outward).

112　カンクウダイ　KANKUDAI

61 挙動	62 挙動
東　　East	東　　East

北から見る
⑩ seen from north.

騎馬立ち。	八字立ち。
Kibadachi	Hachijidachi
⑩のまま。	両足を同時に引き寄せ、膝を伸ばして八字立ち。
same as in ⑩.	Pulling both feet together at once, stretch knees.
右拳落し突き。左拳はそのまま（右拳を左拳の後ろに手首が交差するように）。（左手首が上になる）、右拳甲外。	両掌上段交差受け。
Right fist Otoshitsuki. Left fist same as in ⑩. Cross both hands, with left wrist on top of right wrist and back of right fist faces outside.	Jodan-Kosauke with both palms above head
	交差受けは少し肘を曲げるぐらいで良い。勢いがついている箇所なので膝を強く伸ばしたり、踵を上げたりしないこと。
	Kosauke should be done with a little bending of both elbows. As it is a powerful move, knees must not be overly straightened nor heels be lifted.

113

63 挙動

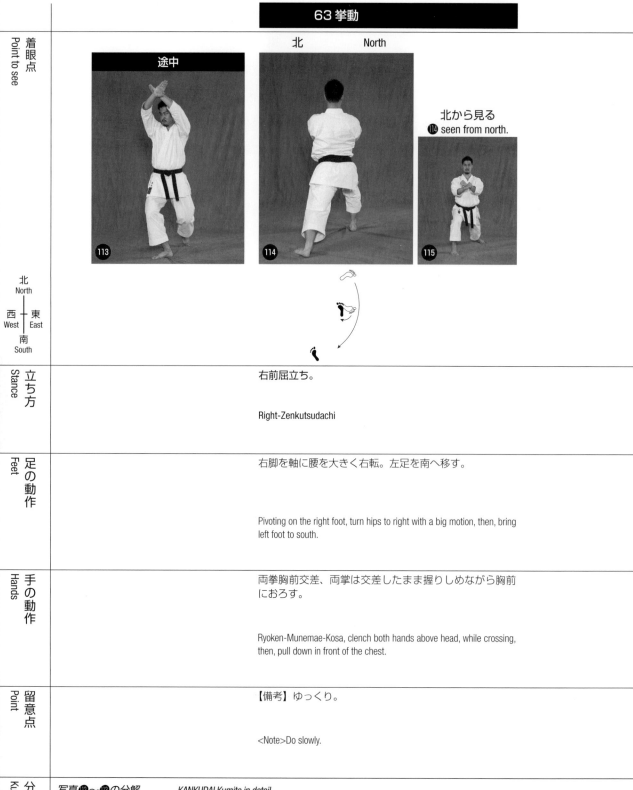

着眼点 / Point to see	北 North / 北から見る seen from north.
立ち方 / Stance	右前屈立ち。 Right-Zenkutsudachi
足の動作 / Feet	右脚を軸に腰を大きく右転。左足を南へ移す。 Pivoting on the right foot, turn hips to right with a big motion, then, bring left foot to south.
手の動作 / Hands	両拳胸前交差、両掌は交差したまま握りしめながら胸前におろす。 Ryoken-Munemae-Kosa, clench both hands above head, while crossing, then, pull down in front of the chest.
留意点 / Point	【備考】ゆっくり。 <Note>Do slowly.
分解 / Kumite in detail	写真⑫〜⑬の分解　KANKUDAI Kumite in detail  上段交差受けをした後、両掌を中心に体を右に回し相手の手首をつかんで両手をさげ、右肩で相手の逆をとる。 After blocking with Jyodan-Kosauke, turn body to right with both palms on the center line. Pull down hands, while grabbing opponent's right wrist, then, apply "Gyaku" to his upper arm with right shoulder.

64 挙動

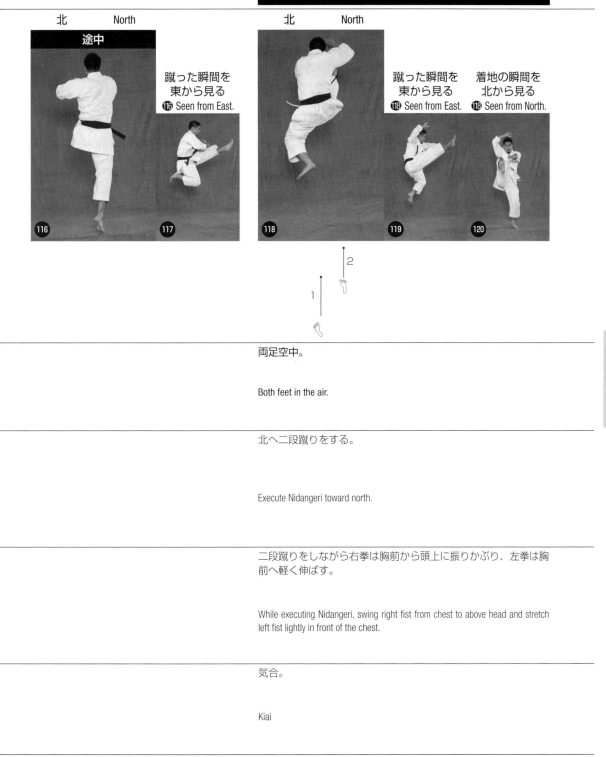

両足空中。

Both feet in the air.

北へ二段蹴りをする。

Execute Nidangeri toward north.

二段蹴りをしながら右拳は胸前から頭上に振りかぶり、左拳は胸前へ軽く伸ばす。

While executing Nidangeri, swing right fist from chest to above head and stretch left fist lightly in front of the chest.

気合。

Kiai

65 挙動

着眼点 Point to see	北　　　North 121　 122 北から見る ⑫ seen from north. 北 North 西 West ＋ 東 East 南 South	途中 123　 124 ⑫から⑫までの途中 Movement between ⑫ and ⑫

立ち方 Stance	右前屈立ち。 Right-Zenkutsudachi
足の動作 Feet	両足（右足前に）着地させる。 Land with both feet (right foot in front).
手の動作 Hands	右裏拳縦回し打ち。左拳左腰に引く。 Right-Uraken-Tatemawashiuchi. Pull back left fist to the left hip.
留意点 Point	右前屈立ちと右裏拳縦回し打ちは同時に決まるように。 Right-Zenkutsudachi and Right-Uraken-Tatemawashiuchi should be performed at the same time.	【備考】ゆっくり。 <Note>Do slowly.
分解 Kumite in detail		

116　カンクウダイ　KANKUDAI

止め	直立
南　　　South	南　　　South

八字立ち。	結び立ち。
Hachijidachi	Musubidachi
右脚を軸に体を右回り、左足を東へ移し八字立ちとなる。 Pivoting on the right foot, turn body to the right, then, Hachijidachi by bringing left foot toward east.	左足、右足の順に閉じ、結び立ち。 Move the left foot, then the right foot, into Musubidachi.
右腕で下段を内から払うように回しながら左右両拳を大きく円を描いて回し、内側に交差しながら静かにおろし自然体にもどる（⑫の姿勢は止めないで自然にもどす）。 Turn right arm from Gedan in a sweeping motion from inside, draw a large circle with both fists, then, after crossing inward, drop hands slowly and returning to the original position (⑫ Shows form during the move. Do not stop at this point, return naturally to the standing Yame position).	両手は開いて大腿部両側に付けて伸ばす。 Open both hands and stretch arms and fingers on both sides of the things.
【備考】止めの時残心に、心がける。 <Note>At Yame position, a state of alertness is important.	

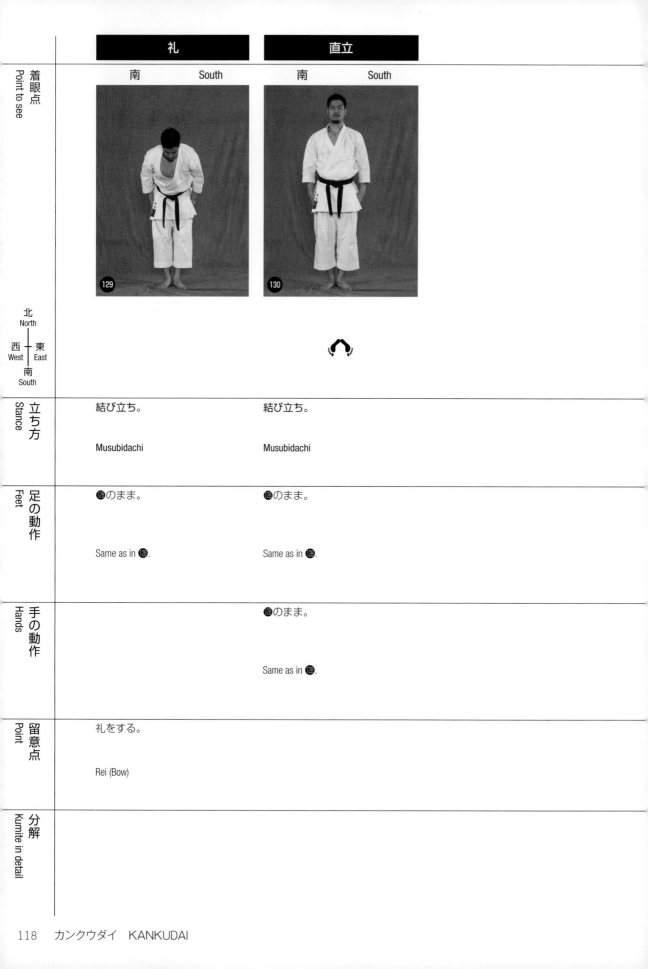

カンクウダイ

バッサイダイ
BASSAIDAI

特徴

バッサイダイは首里手の系統の形であり、基本技が集約され、攻防技の動作が連続的に組み合わされている。
軽快な動きのなかに、技の切り返し、強弱の使い方、敏速な極め技等の流れが求められる。

BASSAIDAI is a KATA of Syuri-te system summing up basic techniques with combination of attack and defense in serial movement.
In the agile movements, counterattack, hard and soft strength and swift decisive techniques must be mastered.

※従来の中段横受けを、中段外受けに、中段横打ち受けを、中段内受けに統一した。
※The names have been consolidated so that what was once known as Chudan-Yokouke is now Chudan-Sotouke, and Chudan-Yoko-Uchi-Uke is now Chudan-Uchiuke.

	直立	礼	直立
	南　　South	南　　South	南　　South
	 ❶	 ❷	 ❸

北 North
西 West ／ 東 East
南 South

着眼点 Point to see			
立ち方 Stance	結び立ち。 Musubidachi	結び立ち。 Musubidachi	結び立ち。 Musubidachi
足の動作 Feet	結び立ち。 Musubidachi	❶のまま。 Same as in ❶.	❶のまま。 Same as in ❶.
手の動作 Hands	両手は開いて大腿部両側に付けて伸ばす。 Open both hands and stretch arms down to both sides of thighs.		❶のまま。 Same as in ❶.
留意点 Point		礼をする。 Rei (Bow)	
分解 Kumite in detail			

122　バッサイダイ　BASSAIDAI

用意	1 挙動
南　　　South	南　　　South
	 　西から見る　❻ seen from west.
閉足立ち。	右交差立ち。
Heisokudachi	Right-Kosadachi
直立姿勢の位置で爪先をつける。	右足を南方へ1歩踏み出し左足を右足へ引きつける。
Without changing upright position, put toes together.	Take right foot one step toward south, then, pull left foot to the right foot.
右拳は軽く握り、左手は開いて右手を包み下腹部に構える。	右手で中段外受けを行い、左手は開いて右拳の内側より掌にて押すようにして添える（右中段拳支え受け）。
Clench right fist lightly and wrapping right fist with left palm, hold them in front of the lower abdomen.	While executing Chudan-Sotouke with right fist, place left hand on right fist as if pressing with palm from inside (Right-Chudan-Kensasaeuke).

写真❺の分解　　BASSAIDAI Kumite in detail

構え姿勢。
中段突きを、斜め後方に前足を引いて右中段拳支え受け。

Kamae posture.
When opponent attacks with Right-Chudantsuki, pull front foot diagonally backward and execute Chudan-Kensasaeuke with right fist.

左手で相手の腕を押さえ右拳で上段へ裏打ちする。

While holding his right arm with left hand, execute Jyodan-Urauchi with right fist.

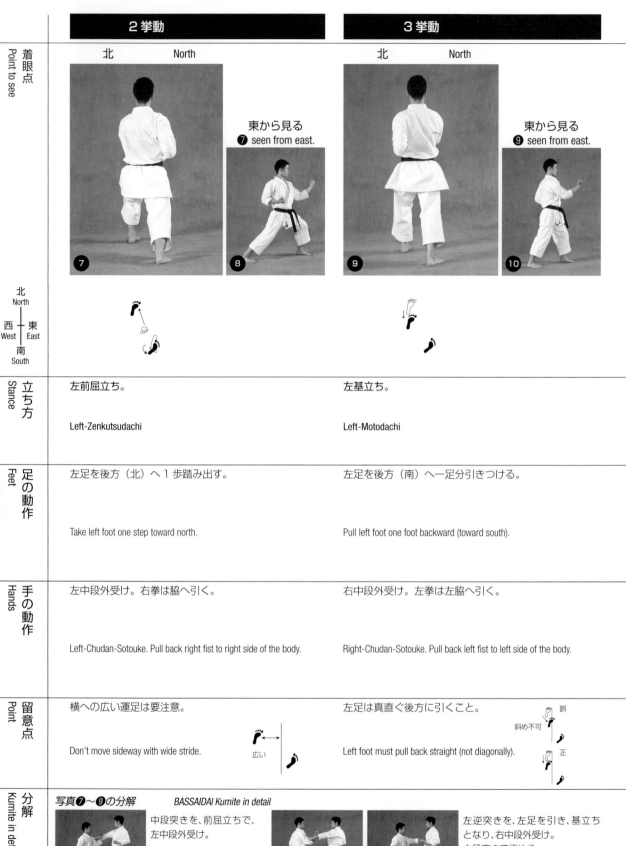

	2 挙動	3 挙動
着眼点 / Point to see	北 North / 東から見る ⑦ seen from east.	北 North / 東から見る ⑨ seen from east.
立ち方 / Stance	左前屈立ち。 Left-Zenkutsudachi	左基立ち。 Left-Motodachi
足の動作 / Feet	左足を後方（北）へ 1 歩踏み出す。 Take left foot one step toward north.	左足を後方（南）へ一足分引きつける。 Pull left foot one foot backward (toward south).
手の動作 / Hands	左中段外受け。右拳は脇へ引く。 Left-Chudan-Sotouke. Pull back right fist to right side of the body.	右中段外受け。左拳は左脇へ引く。 Right-Chudan-Sotouke. Pull back left fist to left side of the body.
留意点 / Point	横への広い運足は要注意。 Don't move sideway with wide stride.	左足は真直ぐ後方に引くこと。 Left foot must pull back straight (not diagonally).

分解 / Kumite in detail

写真❼〜❾の分解　　BASSAIDAI Kumite in detail

中段突きを、前屈立ちで、左中段外受け。

When opponent attacks with Right-Chudantsuki, shift body diagonally backward to right side and execute Left-Chudan-Sotouke.

左逆突きを、左足を引き、基立ちとなり、右中段外受け。中段突きで極める。

Block his further Left-Gyakutsuki with Right-Chudan-Sotouke by Motodachi with drawing back left foot. Counter and finish with Left-Chudantsuki.

バッサイダイ　BASSAIDAI

4 挙動 | 5 挙動

南　South | 南　South

❶ seen from east. | ❸ seen from east.

 |

右前屈立ち。 | 右基立ち。

Right-Zenkutsudachi | Right-Motodachi

右足を後方（南）へ踏み出す。 | 右足を後方（北）へ一足分引く。

Step right foot backward (toward south). | Pull right foot one foot backward (toward north).

左中段内受け。右拳は脇へ引く。 | 右中段外受け。左拳は脇へ引く。

Left-Chudan-Uchiuke. Pull right fist to right side of the body. | Right-Chudan-Sotouke. Pull back left fist to left side of the body.

| ❼～❾に同じ、運足に留意のこと。

| Same as in ❼-❾. Pay attention to foot movement.

写真⓫～⓭の分解　　BASSAIDAI Kumite in detail

 中段突きを、前屈立ちとなり、中段内受け。
Block opponent's Right-Chudantsuki by hitting with Right-Chudan-Uchiuke, while pulling body diagonally backward to Zenkutsudachi.

  中段逆突きを、左足を引き、基立ちとなり、左中段外受け。
中段突きで極める。
Block his further Left-Chudan-Gyakutsuki with Motodachi by drawing back left foot and Left-Chudan-Sotouke. Counter with Right-Chudantsuki.

6 挙動

	南　　　South	西　　　West
着眼点 Point to see	⑮（途中） ⑯ 西から見る ⑮ seen from west.	⑰ ⑱ 西から見る ⑰ seen from west. 右拳は耳の高さ。 Right fist is at the ear level height.
立ち方 Stance	四股立ち。 Shikodachi	八字立ち。 Hachijidachi.
足の動作 Feet	右足を後方（北）へ引いて四股立ちとなる。 Pull right foot backward (toward north) to hold Shikodachi.	右足を左足に引き寄せて八字立ちとなる。 Pull right foot toward left foot to become Hachijidachi.
手の動作 Hands	右腕で下方より掬いあげる。 Scoop upward with right arm.	右腕にて下より掬い上げるようにして上にあげる。右拳の高さは右耳の高さとする。 Raise right arm from underneath as if scooping upward. Right fist is at the ear level height.
留意点 Point	【備考】この動作は掬い止めへの移行動作であり、連続して行う。 <Note>This movement is a serial switchover movement to scoop upward (Sukuidome).	右手で下より掬いあげ、八字立ちになると同時に西を見る。それまでは南を見る。 Scooping upward with right arm from beneath and becoming Hachijidachi, with facing west. Until then, look toward south.

分解　Kumite in detail

写真⑮〜⑰の分解　　BASSAIDAI Kumite in detail

右中段蹴りを、斜め左前方へ入りながら右前腕で掬い。左手で左頸部へ左拳槌にて差し込む。
Catch the opponent's Right-Chudangeri by scooping the right forearm under the leg, while closing distance from the left side. Apply left Hammerfist to the left side of the opponent's neck.

右前腕で足を上にあげ、頸部を下に押さえ。
左足を引いて相手を倒す。
Lift the opponent's foot using the right forearm and press down on the neck. Pull back the left leg to throw the opponent.

126　バッサイダイ　BASSAIDAI

7挙動	8挙動	9挙動
西 West	西 West	南 South

右猫足立ち。	右猫足立ち。	八字立ち。
Right-Nekoashidachi	Right-Nekoashidachi	Hachijidachi
右足の踵を浮かせて前へ出し、腰を落とす。	⓭のまま。	右足を左へ移動し、両上足底を軸にして八字立ちとなる。
Lift right heel and step right foot forward, then, lower hips.	Same as in ⓭.	Pivoting both foot soles after right foot moved toward left to Hachijidachi.
右中段内受け、左拳はそのまま。	左中段外受け、右拳は脇へ引く。	右拳は脇へ引き、左腕は拳の甲を上にして前腕を水平にして水月の前に構える（右脇構え）。
Right-Chudan-Uchiuke, left fist is held right there.	Left-Chudan-Sotouke. Pull back right fist to right side of the body.	Pull back right fist to right side of the body. Put left forearm in front of solar plexus horizontally, with back of left and facing upward(Right-Waki-Kamae).
猫足立ちを崩さないこと。		猫足立ちから八字立ちにかわる場合の歩幅に注意。⓴～㉑動作への移り
Keep up Nekoashidachi.		Pay attention to the width of steps in the actions from Nekoashidachi to Hachijidachi (⓴ to ㉑).

腰を落として突く。

Lower hips and finish with Right-Tsuki, when he is thrown to the ground.

写真⓳～⓴の分解　　BASSAIDAI Kumite in detail

中段突きを、猫足立ちとなり、中段内受け。

Block opponent's Right-Chudantsuki by hitting sideways with Right-Chudan-Uchiuke, while taking Nekoashidachi stance.

	10 挙動	11 挙動
着眼点 Point to see	南 South   ⑳ 東から見る ㉓ seen from east. 左横払いは肩の高さ。 Left-Yokobarai is at height of shoulder.	南 South  ㉔
立ち方 Stance		八字立ち。 Hachijidachi
足の動作 Feet	上足底を軸に踵を動かし、爪先を南西に向ける。両足がやや平行となる。 Pivoting on the balls of the feet, move the heels and point toes towards Southwest. Feet should be approximately parallel.	上足底を軸に㉑にもどす。 Pivoting on the balls of the feet, return the feet to as they were in position ㉑.
手の動作 Hands	左腕にて横に打ち払う（左中段横払い）。 Hit sideways with left arm (Left-Chudan-Yokobarai).	右中段突き、左拳は脇へ引く。 Right-Chudantsuki. Pull back left fist to left side of body.
留意点 Point	【備考】両足爪先を南西に向けると同時に上体を半身にする。 <Note> While both toes pointing toward southwest, upper body become Hanmi.	
分解 Kumite in detail	さらに中段逆突きで攻撃してくるのを、左中段外受け。 Block his further Left-Chudan-Gyakutsuki with Left-Chudan-Uke.	基立ちになり、右中段突き。 Taking Motodachi stance, counter with Right-Chudantsuki.

北 North / 西 West / 東 East / 南 South

128　バッサイダイ　BASSAIDAI

12 挙動	13 挙動
南　　South	南　　South

	八字立ち。 Hachijidachi
上足底を軸に踵を動かし、爪先を南東に向ける。両足は南東に向かってやや平行となる。 Pivoting on the balls of the feet, move the heels and point toes towards Southeast. Feet should be approximately parallel.	上足底を軸に㉔にもどす。 Pivoting on the balls of the feet, return the feet to as they were in position ㉔.
右中段外受けを行う。 Right-Chudan-Sotouke	左中段突き、右拳は脇へ引く。 Left-Chudantsuki. Pull back right fist to right side of body.
腰の回転に乗せながら右中段受けにかわる。右拳を引くだけで受けに変わるのは不可。 【備考】中段受けを行うと同時に上体は半身となる。㉔㉕は連続動作。 Change into Right-Chudan-Uke with body turn. Don't change into Right-Chudan-Uke with pulling back right fist only. <Note>While executing Chudan-Uke, upper body becomes Hanmi. ㉔ and ㉕ must be a continuous movement.	

写真㉒～㉗の分解　　BASSAIDAI Kumite in detail

 中段突きを、右拳槌および前腕で横に打ち払う。

Block opponent's Right-Chudantsuki by scooping his leg with right forearm, while stepping in forward to left side.

 左中段突きを、右中段付きで突き受け。

Block his further Left-Chudantsuki and counter attack with Right-Chudantsuki from beneath.

14 挙動

	南　South	南　South
着眼点 Point to see	 　東から見る ㉘ seen from east. ㉘　㉙	途中  ㉚
北 North 西 West ― 東 East 南 South		
立ち方 Stance		右猫足立ち Right-Nekoashidachi
足の動作 Feet	上足底を軸に踵を動かし、爪先を南西に向ける。両足がやや平行となる。 Pivoting on the balls of the feet, move the heels and point toes towards Southwest. Feet should be approximately parallel.	右足を前方へ出す。 Step forward with the right foot.
手の動作 Hands	左中段外受けを行う。 Left-Chudan-Sotouke.	右手を開いて、甲を下にして体の前から前腕を水平にする。 Open right hand, back of hand facing downward, and hold forearm in front of chest horizontally.
留意点 Point		
分解 Kumite in detail	中段突きを、右中段外受け。 Block his further Right-Chudantsuki with Right-Chudan-Sotouke.	　左中段突き。 Counter with Left-Chudantsuki.

130　バッサイダイ　BASSAIDAI

	15 挙動	16 挙動	17 挙動
	南 South	南 South	南 South
	㉛	㉜	㉝
	右猫足立ち。	左猫足立ち。	右猫足立ち。
	Right-Nekoashidachi	Left-Nekoashidachi	Right-Nekoashidachi
	㉚のまま。	左足を南へ出す。	右足を南へ出す。
	Same as in ㉚.	Step out left foot toward south.	Step out right foot toward south.
	右手刀下段払い、左手は開いて甲を下に向け水月前に引く。	左手刀下段払い、右手は水月前に引く。	右手刀下段払い、左手は水月前に引く。
	Gedanbarai with Right-Shuto. Open left hand, with back of hand facing downward, and pull it in front of solar plexus.	While executing Gedanbarai with Left-Shuto, pull up right hand in front of solar plexus.	While executing Gedanbarai with Right-Shuto, pull up left hand in front of solar plexus.
	㉘〜㉛最短距離を通って一挙動で動く。		
	Hands of ㉘ - ㉛ must move in one action by shortest route.		

写真㉛〜㉝の分解　　BASSAIDAI Kumite in detail

中段蹴りを、猫足立ちとなり、左手刀下段払い。

Block opponent's Right-Chudangeri with Left-Shuto-Gedanbarai, while withdrawing body diagonally to right side and taking Nekoashidachi stance.

右中段突きを、左中段掛け手。

Block his further Right-Chudantsuki with Left-Chudan-Kakete.

	18挙動	19挙動
着眼点 Point to see	南 South 	南 South  東から見る ㉟ seen from east.  上半身のみを半身になり左猫足立ちが崩れないこと。 Hold left Nekoashidachi firmly with Hanmi position by upper body only.
北 North / 西 West / 東 East / 南 South		
立ち方 Stance	左猫足立ち。 Left-Nekoashidachi	左猫足立ち。 Left-Nekoashidachi
足の動作 Feet	右足を後ろ（北）へ引く。 Pull right foot backward (toward north).	㉞のまま。 Same as in ㉞.
手の動作 Hands	左中段掛け手、右手は甲を上にして水月前に引く。 Left-Chudan-Kakete. Pull up right hand, back of hand facing upward, in front of solar plexus.	左手をすこし下にさげてから中段掛け手を行いながら左胸（乳）まで引き、右手は開手で体の左側前に出して流し受けをする。 Lower left hand slightly and, while executing Chudan-Kakete, pull it to left chest, push right hand, with palm open, forward in front of left side of body and execute Nagashiuke.
留意点 Point		左右の手の動作は同時に行い、上体は半身となる。左掛け手をそのまま中段に引き付けてはならない。 Movement of both hands must be done simultaneously. Upper body become Hanmi. Don't pull Left-Kakete directly to Chudan.
分解 Kumite in detail	 左中段逆突きで攻撃してくるのを、左手を相手の突きの下より回して、掛け手で手首を捕り、右手で流し受けを行う。 Block his further Left-Chudan-Gyakutsuki by grasping his wrist with Kakete after moving left hand around his left hand, then, execute Nagashiuke with right hand.	

20 挙動

南　South

途中

東から見る
❸ seen from east.

❸❼　❸❽

南　South

東から見る
❸ seen from east.

❸❾　❹⓿

	八字立ち。 Hachijidachi
左足踵を下につけ、右足を左足の膝の上まであげる。 While placing left heel firmly on the floor, lift right knee until the heel reaches knee height.	右の足刀を前（南）へ踏みおろす。 Put down right Sokuto forward (toward south).
❸のまま。 Same as in ❸.	両手を握り、甲を上にして左腰の脇へ引きつける。 Clenching both hands, back of hands facing upward, pull them to left hip.
右足をあげたときに爪先を上に反らす。❸から❸への移行動作。 When lifting right knee, bend toe upward. Transition movement from ❸ to ❸.	左脇をしっかりと締めて引き付けること。 Pull back arms in squeezing to left side of body.

相手の腕を捕ると同時に、右足を上にあげ。

While grasping his left arm with right hand, lift right knee.

足刀を相手の膝の内側に当て、踏みおろす。

Strike his inside of right knee with Sokuto of lifted right foot.

	21 挙動	22 挙動
着眼点 Point to see	北　North 北から見る ㊶ seen from north. ㊶ ㊷	北　North 北から見る ㊸ seen from north. ㊸ ㊹
北 North 西 West ｜ 東 East 南 South		
立ち方 Stance	左猫足立ち。 Left-Nekoashidachi	右猫足立ち Right-Nekoashidachi
足の動作 Feet	後ろ（北）へ向き、左足をすこし引く。 Turn around body backward (toward north) and pull back left foot slightly.	右足を半歩前へ出す。 Take right foot half step forward.
手の動作 Hands	左中段手刀受け、右手は水月前に引く。 Left-Chudan-Shutouke. Pull right hand in front of solar plexus.	右中段手刀受け。左手は水月前に引く。 Right-Chudan-Shutouke. Pull left hand in front of solar plexus.
留意点 Point		
分解 Kumite in detail	写真㊶〜㊿の分解　　*BASSAIDAI Kumite in detail* 中段突きを、猫足立ちとなり、手刀受け。 Block opponent's Right-Chudantsuki with Left-Shutouke, while withdrawing body diagonally to right side and taking Nekoashidachi stance.	

134　バッサイダイ　BASSAIDAI

23 挙動	24 挙動
北 North	北 North

閉足立ち。	右前屈立ち。
Heisokudachi	Right-Zenkutsudachi
右足を左足へ引きつける。	右足を1歩踏み出す。
Pull right foot to left foot.	Take right foot a step forward.
上段輪受け。右手を引きつけ、両拳・両肘を締めながら上段輪受けに入る。上段輪受けのとき、肘を曲げること。	左右の拳槌を中段へ打ち込む。
Execute Jyodan-Wauke. Pulling back right hand, bring both fists and elbows together to enter the movement. When doing Jyodan-Wauke, make sure to keep the elbows bent.	Hit toward Chudan with Right and Left-Kentsui.
	1歩踏み込んだときは、確実に前屈立ちになること。
	When taking one step forward, stand Zenkutsudachi firmly.

左上段逆突きを、上段輪受け。

Block his further Left-Jyodan-Gyakutsuki with Jyodan-Wauke, bringing up both hands.

右足を1歩踏み込んで左右の拳槌で脇腹へ打ち込む。

Take right foot in a step toward opponent, then, hit at his both sides of body with both Kentsui.

25 挙動	26 挙動

着眼点 / Point to see

北　North　| 南　South

50

西から見る
50 seen from west.
51

52

西から見る
52 seen from west.
53

北 North
西 West ＋ 東 East
南 South

立ち方 / Stance

四股立ち。

Shikodachi

閉足立ち。

Heisokudachi

足の動作 / Feet

両足を前（北）へすこしずらして進める。

Move both feet forward a little.

左足を右足へつける。

Pull left foot to right foot together.

手の動作 / Hands

右拳で中段突き、左拳は脇へ引く。

Chudantsuki with right fist. Pull back left fist to left side of the body.

左下段払い、右拳は耳の高さに構える。

Left-Gedanbarai. Hold right fist on level of right ear height.

留意点 / Point

【備考】右拳の中段突きは肩の高さと同じ位置。直ちに四股立ちに転ずる。この時右方向（北）に少し寄り足。

<Note>Chudantsuki with right fist must be on level of shoulder height. Change into Shikodachi immediately with dragging a little toward north (Yoriashi).

左右の前腕は体の中央で交差して、下段払いおよび構えを行う。四股立ちから、閉足立ち・上段・下段の動作は一挙動。ゆっくりは不可。

After crossing both forearms in front of abdomen, execute Gedanbarai and Kamae. Movement from Shikodachi to Heisokudachi, Jyodan and Gedan must be done in a stroke. Slow movement must not be done.

分解 / Kumite in detail

相手が体を後ろへ引いて拳槌打ちをかわしたら、四股立ちで踏み込み、右中段突きで極める。
If opponent pulls back body to dodge Kentsuiuchi, then, step in to become Shikodachi and finish with Right-Chudantsuki.

写真52～54の分解　　*BASSAIDAI Kumite in detail*

中段突きを、左下段払い。

Block opponent's Right-Chudantsuki with Left-Gedanbarai.

136　バッサイダイ　BASSAIDAI

27 挙動 — 南 / South

 東から見る ❺ seen from east.

四股立ち。

Shikodachi

右足を前（南）へ1歩踏み出して腰を落とす。

Take right foot one step forward (toward south), then, lower hips.

右下段払い、左手は甲を上にして水月の高さに水平に構える。

Right-Gedanbarai. Hold left forearm in front of solar plexus horizontally, with back of left hand facing upward.

28 挙動 — 北 / North

 東から見る ❺ seen from east.

左基立ち。

Left-Motodachi

後ろ（北）へ体を向け、左足をすこし引きつける。

Turn around body backward (toward north) and pull back left foot slightly.

左中段横払い、右拳は脇へ引く。

Hit Left-Chudan-Yokobarai with left fist. Pull back right fist to right side of the body.

左中段蹴りを、四股立ちとなり、右下段払い。

Block his further Left-Chudangeri with Right-Gedanbarai, while withdrawing front foot diagonally to left side and taking Shikodachi stance.

中段突き。

Counter with Left-Chudantsuki.

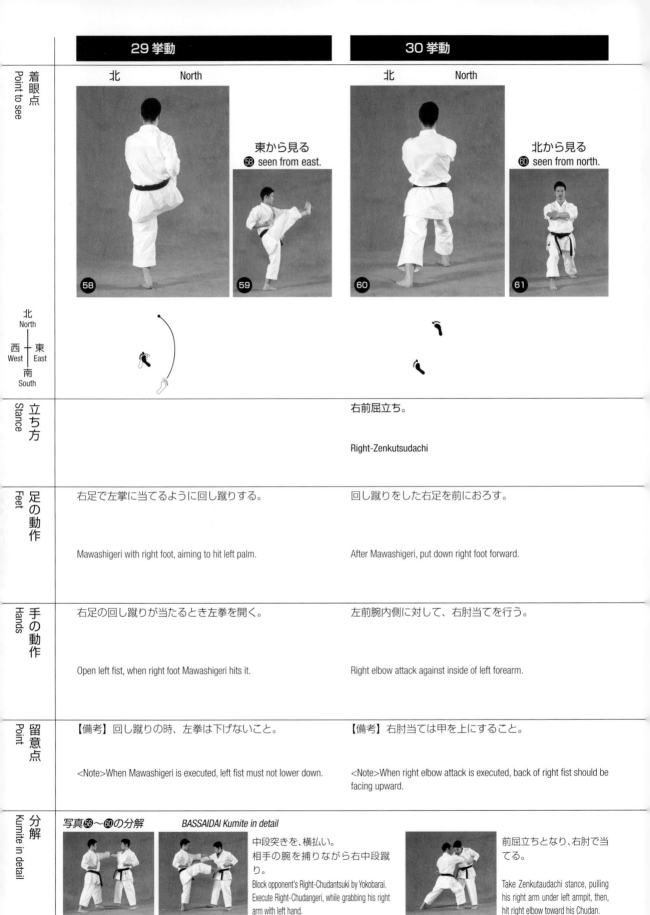

31 挙動	32 挙動
北　North	北　North

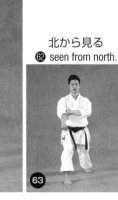

北から見る ❻ seen from north.　　北から見る ❻ seen from north.

右前屈立ち。	右前屈立ち。
Right-Zenkutsudachi	Right-Zenkutsudachi
❻のまま。	❻のまま。
Same as in ❻.	Same as in ❻.
肘当てをした右手で下段払い、左拳は右肘関節の内側に構える。	左下段払い、右拳は左肘の内側へ構える。
After elbow attack, execute Gedanbarai with right fist. Hold left fist against inside of the right elbow.	Left-Gedanbarai. Hold right fist against inside of left elbow.

3回の下段払いは1・2・3回とも等間隔で行う。

Three times execution of Gedanbarai must be done in a same interval.

写真❻～❼の分解　　BASSAIDAI Kumite in detail

中段突きを、左下段払い。

Block opponent's Right-Chudantsuki with Left-Gedannbarai.

中段突きを、下段に払い。

Block his further Left-Chudantsuki with Right-Gedanbarai.

139

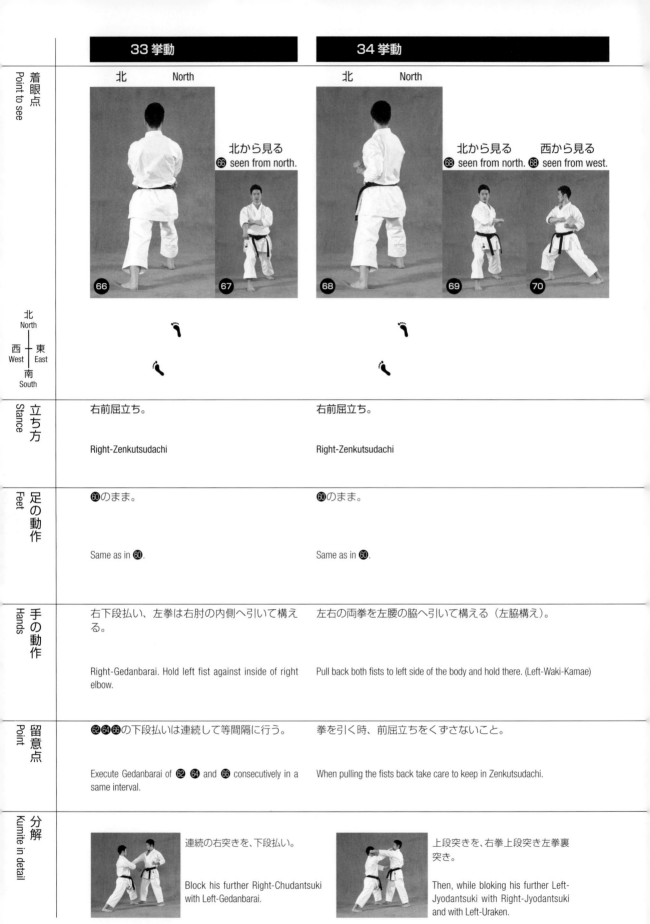

35 挙動

北　　North

西から見る
㉑ seen from west.

右前屈立ち。

Right-Zenkutsudachi

㉠のまま。

Same as in ㉠.

左上段突き、右拳は裏突きで同時に突く（双手突き）。

While executing Left-Jyodantsuki, with execute Right-Uratsuki at the same time (Morotetsuki).

両方の突きは正中線に揃える。双手突きのとき、前屈立ちをくずさないこと。

Both fists should be aligned to the opponent's center line. Take care to remain in Zenkutsudachi when executing Morotetsuki.

36 挙動

北　　North

北から見る
㉓ seen from north.

閉足立ち。

Heisokudachi

右足を左足に引きつける。

Pull right foot to left foot.

左右の拳を右脇へ引いて構える（右脇構え）。

Pull back both fists to right side of the body (Right-Waki-Kamae).

㉑から右足を引き、閉足立ちになるとき左下足底があがらぬこと。

When right foot is pulled back from ㉑ and become Heisokudachi don't lift up left bottom of foot.

141

		37 挙動	38 挙動
着眼点 Point to see		北　　North 北から見る ㊆ seen from north.	北　　North 北から見る ㊆ seen from north.
		北 North 西 ┼ 東 West　East 南 South	
立ち方 Stance		左前屈立ち。 Left-Zenkutsudachi	閉足立ち。 Heisokudachi
足の動作 Feet		左足を北へ1歩踏み出す。 Take left foot one step forward to north.	左足を右足に引きつける。 Pull left foot to right foot.
手の動作 Hands		右上段突き、左拳は裏突きで同時に突く（双手突き）。 While executing Right-Jyodantsuki, with execute Left-Uratsuki at the same time (Morotetsuki).	左右の拳を左脇へ引いて構える（左脇構え）。 Pull back both fists to left side of body (Hidariwaki Kamae).
留意点 Point			
分解 Kumite in detail			

142　バッサイダイ　BASSAIDAI

39 挙動

北　　　　North　　　　　　　　　　　南　　　　South

北から見る
79 seen from north.

途中

右前屈立ち。	前屈立ちのような立ち方。
Right-Zenkutsudachi	Similar to Zenkutsudachi.
右足を北へ１歩踏み出す。	右足を軸にして後方（南）へ体を回す。左膝は曲げ、右足は伸ばして立つ。両爪先は南東へ向く。
Take right foot one step forward to north.	Pivoting on right foot, turn around body backward (toward south). Bend left knee and stretch right leg. Both toes point toward southeast.
左上段突き、右拳は裏突きで同時に突く（双手突き）。	右腕を伸ばし体の左側まで振るようにして払う。
While executing Left-Jyodantsuki, with execute Right-Uratsuki at the same time (Morotetsuki).	Extend the right arm to the left side of the body in a sweeping motion.
⓺⓼〜⓻⓽で下足底をあげないこと。	【備考】腰の回転に乗せながら右拳を大きく振込んで中段振り捨てをする。
Don't lift up bottom of foot from ⓺⓼ to ⓻⓽.	<Note>While turning hips, execute right fist Furikomi-Chudan-Furisute.

40 挙動

	南 South		南 South

東から見る
⑧② seen from east.

途中

北 North
西 West — 東 East
南 South

Stance 立ち方	前屈立ちのような立ち方。 Similar to Zenkutsudachi.		前屈立ちのような立ち方。 Similar to Zenkutsudachi.
Feet 足の動作	⑧①のまま。 Same as in ⑧①.		上足底を軸に両爪先を南西に向け、右膝を曲げ、左膝を伸ばす。 Pivoting on the balls of the feet, move the heels and point toes towards Southwest. The right knee should be bent, and the left leg straight.
Hands 手の動作	払った右腕をただちに体の右側まで返す。この時、前腕は水平にする。(振捨て) Return the right arm directly back to the right side of the body. The forearm should be level to the floor (Furisute).		左腕を伸ばし体の右側まで振るようにして払う。 Extend the left arm to the right side of the body in a sweeping motion.
Point 留意点	【備考】⑧①の手の動作は連続する。このとき右手の甲を下にして前腕は水平とする。⑧①⑧②の前腕を返すとき裏拳で下を打つような要領で止める。 <Note>Hands in ⑧① must be a continuous movement. Back of right hand should be facing downward, while forearm is kept horizontal. When forearm of ⑧①⑧② is turned back, stop it like hitting downward with Uraken.		

Kumite in detail 分解

写真⑧①〜⑧⑤の分解   BASSAIDAI Kumite in detail

中段蹴りを、右前腕で内側に引っ掛け。

When opponent attacks with Right-Chudangeri, pull front foot backward, then, hook his right foot on right forearm.

前腕をかえして。

Turn around right forearm.

バッサイダイ　BASSAIDAI

41 挙動

南　South　　　　　　　　　　　南西　Southwest

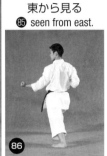

東から見る
⑧⑤ seen from east.

途中

前屈立ちのような立ち方。

Similar to Zenkutsudachi.

❽❹のまま。	左足を半歩斜め後ろへ引く。
Same as in ❽❹.	Pull left foot half step diagonally backward.
払った左前腕を体の左側まで甲を下にして返す。このとき前腕を水平にする（振捨て）。	❽⑤のまま。
Return the left arm directly back to the left side of the body. The forearm should be level to the floor (Furisute).	Same as in ❽⑤.

体の外側に相手の足を振捨てる。

Drop his right foot to right side of body.

背中に中段突き。

Counter immediately with Chudantsuki to his exposed back.

145

42 挙動

Point to see 着眼点	南西 Southwest	南東 Southeast	南東 Southeast
	 ⑧⑧	途中  ⑧⑨	途中  ⑨⓪

北 North / 西 West — 東 East / 南 South

立ち方 Stance	右猫足立ち。 Right-Nekoashidachi	右猫足立ち。 Right-Nekoashidachi	
足の動作 Feet	腰を落として右足踵をあげて左足方向へ引く。 Lower down hips, lift right foot heel and pull toward left foot.	⑧⑧のまま。 Same as in ⑧⑧.	右足を左足の斜め後方（北西）へ引く。 Pull back right foot to back of left foot diagonally (toward northwest).
手の動作 Hands	右中段掛け手。左手は甲を上にして水月前に構える。 Chudan-Kakete with right hand. Hold left hand in front of solar plexus, back of hand facing upward.	⑧⑧のまま。 Same as in ⑧⑧.	両手を右足を引いた方向（北西）へ⑧⑨の高さのまま引く。 Pull back both hand with ⑧⑨ height toward northwest, together with right foot.
留意点 Point		【備考】目付けだけ南東に向ける。 <Note> No change in position except for looking towards Southeast.	【備考】右足を引いた時、爪先は南に向けておく。 <Note> When pulling back the left foot, keep the toes pointing South.

分解 Kumite in detail

写真⑧⑧〜⑨① の分解　　*BASSAIDAI Kumite in detail*

 中段突きを、猫足立ちとなり、掛け手。

Block opponent's Right-Chudantsuki with Right-Kakete, while withdrawing front foot diagonally to left side and taking Nekoashidachi stance.

 相手の手首を捕り。

Grab his right wrist with right hand.

146　バッサイダイ　BASSAIDAI

43 挙動		止め
南東　Southeast	南東　Southeast	南　South

残心

左猫足立ち。	閉足立ち。	閉足立ち。
Left-Nekoashidachi	Heisokudachi	Heisokudachi
引いた右足の踵をつけ、左足踵をあげ、右足の方向へすこし引く。	左足を右足に引きつける。	92のまま。
Put down right heel, lift left heel and pull left foot to right foot slightly.	Pull left foot to right foot together.	Same as in 92.
左中段掛け手。右手は甲を上にして水月前に構える。	右手は握り、左手は開いて右拳を包み、下腹部に構える。	
Chudan-Kakete with left hand. Hold right hand facing upward in front of solar plexus.	Clench right hand while wrapping right fist with left palm and hold them in front of the lower abdomen.	
		南東より残心後、南。
		After keeping Zanshin (a state of alertness after a technique) toward Southeast, turn head to face directly south.

前足で中段蹴りする。

Chudangeri with front foot.

左中段突き。

Put down kicking right foot forward, then, execute Left-Chudantsuki to his right side of body.

147

	直立	礼	直立
着眼点 Point to see	南　　South 94	南　　South 95	南　　South 96
北 North 西 West ― 東 East 南 South			
立ち方 Stance	結び立ち。 Musubidachi	結び立ち。 Musubidachi	結び立ち。 Musubidachi
足の動作 Feet	両爪先を開く。 Open both toes.	**94**のまま。 Same as in **94**.	**94**のまま。 Same as in **94**.
手の動作 Hands	両手は開いて大腿部両側に付けて 伸ばす。 Open both hands and stretch arms down to both sides of thighs.		**94**のまま。 Same as in **94**.
留意点 Point		礼をする。 Rei (Bow)	
分解 Kumite in detail			

148　バッサイダイ　BASSAIDAI

サイファ

セーパイ

ジオン

カンクウダイ

バッサイダイ

セイエンチン

セイシャン

チントウ

セイエンチン
SEIENCHIN

特徴

セイエンチンは那覇手の系統の形であり、接近戦法が多く組み合わされ、蹴り技がなく、重厚な動きに特徴がある。
演武線は左右対をなし、同一の動作が多く、呼吸と動作の緩急が一致している。

SEIENCHIN is a part of Naha-Te Schools, featured of its solid movement in wellcombined infighting tactics without Keriwaza.
Enbusen is paired with right and left, performs same movement often and lenience and severity are harmonized in respiration and movements.

※従来の中段横受けを、中段外受けに、中段横打ち受けを、中段内受けに統一した。
※The names have been consolidated so that what was once known as Chudan-Yokouke is now Chudan-Sotouke, and Chudan-Yoko-Uchi-Uke is now Chudan-Uchiuke.

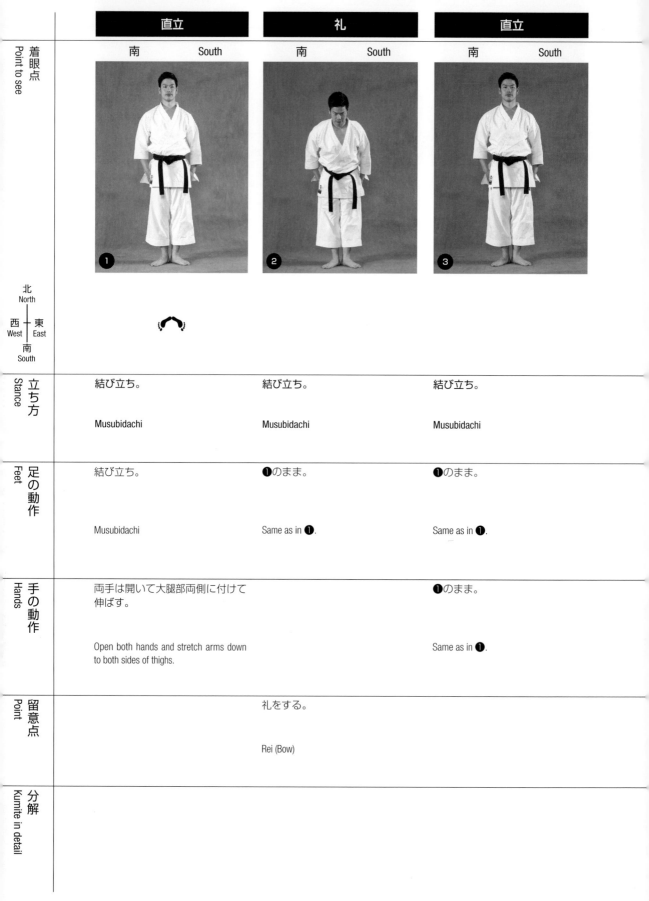

		直立	礼	直立
着眼点 Point to see		南 South ①	南 South ②	南 South ③
立ち方 Stance		結び立ち。 Musubidachi	結び立ち。 Musubidachi	結び立ち。 Musubidachi
足の動作 Feet		結び立ち。 Musubidachi	❶のまま。 Same as in ❶.	❶のまま。 Same as in ❶.
手の動作 Hands		両手は開いて大腿部両側に付けて伸ばす。 Open both hands and stretch arms down to both sides of thighs.		❶のまま。 Same as in ❶.
留意点 Point			礼をする。 Rei (Bow)	
分解 Kumite in detail				

152　セイエンチン　SEIENCHIN

	用意	1 挙動
南　　　South	南　　　South	南　　　South

結び立ち。 Musubidachi	結び立ち。 Musubidachi	平行立ち。 Heikodachi
❶のまま。 Same as in ❶.	❶のまま。 Same as in ❶.	両足の爪先を軸にして両足踵を爪先の間隔に開き両足を平行にする。 Pivoting on the tips of toes, move both heels until parallel.
両手は開き、左掌に右甲を重ね、腹部前に上げる。 Open both hands, placing the back of the right hand on top of the palm of the left, and raise up to in front of the abdomen.	両手を返し、下を押すように構える。 Revolve both hands inward then, as if pushing downward, move into position.	左右の手は握って体側に開き、下にさげ、肩を十分さげて臍下丹田に力を入れる。 Gripping hands and stretch them down along side of the body. Pull down shoulders deeply and concentrate power in the lower abdomen(Seikatanden).

		2 挙動	3 挙動	4 挙動
着眼点 Point to see		南 South	南 South	南 South
		⑦	⑧	⑨
立ち方 Stance		四股立ち。 Shikodachi	四股立ち。 Shikodachi	四股立ち。 Shikodachi
足の動作 Feet		右足を南西へ半円を描きながら踏み出す。 Drawing a semicircle with the right foot, step out towards Southwest.	⑦のまま。 Same as in ⑦.	⑦のまま。 Same as in ⑦.
手の動作 Hands		両手は開いて甲を外に向け、両体側に自然に伸ばす。 Open both hands, back of hands facing outside, and stretch them naturally along side of the body.	左右の手を掬うようにしてゆっくりとあげ、胸の前で両手の甲を合わせる。 Pull up both hands slowly in a scooping motion, then put both back of hands together in front of the chest.	両手を握りながら体の両側へ引っ張るようにゆっくりと下段払いを行う。 Slowly clenching both hands, pull them away from each other, slowly down along side of the body, and execute Gedanbarai.
留意点 Point			⑦〜⑧への動作で肘の狭まりと手の掬い上げは連動すること。両手をあげるとき、肩をあげぬこと。両手と胸との間は、拳一握り分あける。 During movements ⑦ to ⑧, the closing of elbows and scooping motion should happen simultaneously, taking care not to raise shoulders when moving the arms. There should be a fist's width of space between hands and chest.	⑧〜⑨への下段払いが掻き分けにならないように。 Gedanbarai from ⑧ to ⑨ must not be Kakiwake.

分解 Kumite in detail

写真⑦〜㉔の分解　　　*SEIENCHIN Kumite in detail*

構え姿勢。

Kamae posture

中段突きを、左手下段払い。

Withdrawing body toward right diagonally against opponent's Right-Chudantsuki, execute Gedanbarai with left fist.

154　セイエンチン　SEIENCHIN

5挙動	6挙動	7挙動
南　　　South	南　　　South	南　　　South

四股立ち。 Shikodachi	四股立ち。 Shikodachi	四股立ち。 Shikodachi
❼のまま。 Same as in ❼.	❼のまま。 Same as in ❼.	❼のまま。 Same as in ❼.
両手は開いて南へ右中段外受け、左手は甲を下にして水月前に構える。 Open both hands, execute Chudan-Sotouke toward South with right palm, and hold left palm, with the back of hand facing downward, in front of solar plexus.	右手を返して掛け手を行う。 Turn right hand around into Kakete.	掛けた右手を右脇へゆっくり引きながら、左四本貫手で南西方向を突く。 While slowly pulling right Kakete back to the right side, Left hand strikes towards Southwest with Left-four-finger Nukite.
中段外受けは正面（南）に対して行う。 Execute Chudan-Sotouke toward south.	❿⓫の手の動作は連続する。右中段受けからの掛け手は素早くする。肘・手が上下前後に動くのは不可。 Hands in ❿ and ⓫ must be a continuous movement. Kakete from Right-Chudan-Sotouke must act quickly. Elbows and hands must not move up and down or front and back.	動作はゆっくりと行う。引く右手は肘をさげるようにして、肩をぜったいあげぬこと。左貫手の方向は体面に沿って右肘下の方向に突く。 Movements must be acted slowly. Keep right elbow low, when pulling back hand. Never raise right shoulder under any circumstances. The direction of Left-Nukite comes down toward right elbow closely along the body.

中段逆突きを、四股立ちになり、中段外受け。

Block opponent's Left-Chudan-Gyakutsuki with Chudan-Sotouke at Shikodachi by drawing back left foot.

掌をかえして相手の腕を捕る。

Turn round left palm and grab opponent's left arm.

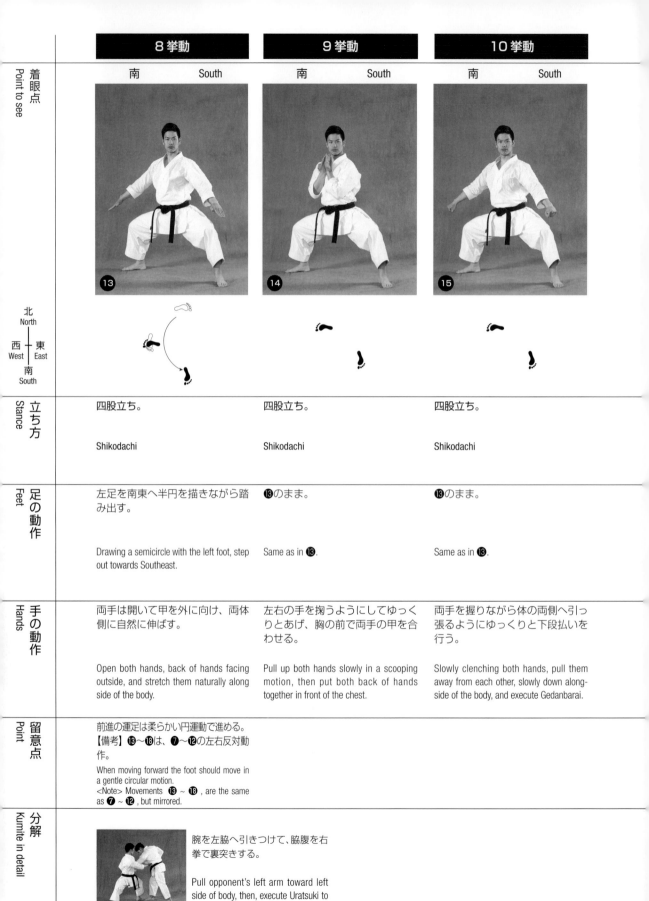

11 挙動	12 挙動	13 挙動
南　　　South	南　　　South	南　　　South

四股立ち。	四股立ち。	四股立ち。
Shikodachi	Shikodachi	Shikodachi
⑬のまま。	⑬のまま。	⑬のまま。
Same as in ⑬.	Same as in ⑬.	Same as in ⑬.
両手は開いて南へ左中段外受け、右手は甲を下にして水月前に構える。	左手を返して掛け手を行う。	掛けた左手を左脇へゆっくり引きながら、右四本貫手で南東方向を突く。
Open both hands, execute Chudan-Sotouke toward South with left palm, and hold right palm, with the back of hand facing downward, in front of solar plexus.	Turn left hand around into Kakete.	While slowly pulling Left-Kakete back to the left side, right hand strikes towards Southeast with Right-four-finger Nukite.

サイファ　セーパイ　ジオン　カンクウダイ　バッサイダイ　**セイエンチン**　セイシャン　チントウ

157

		14 挙動	15 挙動	16 挙動
着眼点 Point to see		南　　South	南　　South	南　　South
		⑲	⑳	㉑
立ち方 Stance		四股立ち。 Shikodachi	四股立ち。 Shikodachi	四股立ち。 Shikodachi
足の動作 Feet		右足を南西へ半円を描きながら踏み出す。 Drawing a semicircle with the right foot, step out towards Southwest.	⑲のまま。 Same as in ⑲.	⑲のまま。 Same as in ⑲.
手の動作 Hands		両手は開いて甲を外に向け、両体側に自然に伸ばす。 Open both hands, back of hands facing outside, and stretch them naturally along side of the body.	左右の手を掬うようにしてゆっくりとあげ、胸の前で両手の甲を合わせる。 Pull up both hands slowly in a scooping motion, then put both back of hands together in front of the chest.	両手を握りながら体の両側へ引っ張るようにゆっくりと下段払いを行う。 Slowly clenching both hands, pull them away from each other, slowly down along-side of the body, and execute Gedanbarai.
留意点 Point		【備考】⑲～㉔は、❼～⓬と同じ動作。 <Note>Movements ⑲ ~ ㉔ are identical to ❼ ~ ⓬ .		
分解 Kumite in detail				

158　セイエンチン　SEIENCHIN

17 挙動	18 挙動	19 挙動
南　　　South	南　　　South	南　　　South
㉒	㉓	㉔
四股立ち。	四股立ち。	四股立ち。
Shikodachi	Shikodachi	Shikodachi
⑲のまま。	⑲のまま。	⑲のまま。
Same as in ⑲.	Same as in ⑲.	Same as in ⑲.
両手は開いて南へ右中段外受け、左手は甲を下にして水月前に構える。	右手を返して掛け手を行う。	掛けた右手を右脇へゆっくり引きながら、左四本貫手で南西方向を突く。
Open both hands, execute Chudan-Sotouke toward South with right palm, and hold left palm, with the back of hand facing downward, in front of solar plexus.	Turn right hand around into Kakete.	While slowly pulling right Kakete back to the right side, Left hand strikes towards Southwest with Left-four-finger Nukite.

サイファ　セーパイ　ジオン　カンクウダイ　バッサイダイ　**セイエンチン**　セイシャン　チントウ

159

	20 挙動	21 挙動
着眼点 Point to see	南　South  ㉕　　㉖ 西から見る ㉕ seen from west.	南　South ㉗　　㉘ 西から見る ㉗ seen from west.
北 North 西 West ／ 東 East 南 South		
立ち方 Stance		右基立ち。 Right-Motodachi
足の動作 Feet	左足に右足を引きつけて片足で立つ。 Pull right foot to left foot and stand on left foot.	右足を前（南）へ踏み込み、左足を寄せる。 Step right foot forward (toward south) and draw up left foot.
手の動作 Hands	左手は開いて掌を上にして水月前に引き、左掌の上に右拳の甲を下にして乗せる。 Pull back left hand in front of solar plexus, with palm facing upward, then, place right fist, back of hand facing downward on top of left palm.	右拳および左手を返して胸の高さで南へ押し込む。 Turn over the right fist together with the left hand and strike in a pushing motion towards South at chest hight.
留意点 Point	㉔〜㉕への移りで「足の動作」の立ちと、左右の手は連動すること。ただし、左右の手は自然に水月前に構える。 While moving from ㉔ to ㉕ standing on foot in Action of Foot and both hands should be moved simultaneously. In this case hold both hands in front of solar plexus.	
分解 Kumite in detail	写真㉕〜㉛の分解　SEIENCHIN Kumite in detail 襟（えり）を捕ってきたとき。 Being grabbed by the collar from front.	 左手を開いて水月前に置き。 Open left hand, place it in front of solar plexus, then, put right fist, back of hand facing downward on top of left palm.

160　セイエンチン　SEIENCHIN

22 挙動	23 挙動
南 South	南 South
  西から見る ㉙ seen from west.	  西から見る ㉛ seen from west.
左基立ち。 Left-Motodachi	左基立ち。 Left-Motodachi
右足を後方へ1歩引く。 Pull right foot one step backward.	㉙のまま。 Same as in ㉙.
右拳は脇へ引き、左手は掌を内に向けて左体側へ伸ばす。 Pull back right fist to right side of the body and stretch left hand straight along left side of the body, with palm facing inside.	左手を中に入れ掌に対し右中段肘当てを行う。 Pull left hand inside and execute Right-Chudan elbow attack against left palm.
	肘当てのとき、腰を入れる。肘当が高くならぬよう留意すること。体の中央部に肘当てを行う。 When executing elbow attack, move right hip in. Pay attention that Hijiate is not executed to upper but centre part of the body.

右拳および左掌をかえして、相手の中心に向かって押し込む。

Turn around right fist and left palm, then, press them against center part of opponent.

両手を突き離すと同時に、右足を踏み込む。

While pushing him away with both hands, step right foot in.

		24 挙動	25 挙動	26 挙動
着眼点 Point to see		南西　Southwest 北西から見る ㉝ seen from northwest. ㉞	南西　Southwest ㉟	南西　Southwest ㊱
	北 North 西 West — 東 East 南 South			
立ち方 Stance		右三戦立ち。 Right-Sanchindachi	四股立ち。 Shikodachi	四股立ち。 Shikodachi
足の動作 Feet		左足を軸にして右足で円を描くようにして南西方向へ右足を1歩運ぶ。 Pivoting on the left foot, bring right foot to southwest as if drawing a circle.	左足を南西方向へ1歩踏み出す。 Take left foot one step toward southwest.	左足を後方へ1歩引く。 Pull left foot one step backward.
手の動作 Hands		左手は開いて右拳槌部に添えて右中段外受けを行う（拳支え受け）。 Execute Chudan-Sotouke (Ken-Sasaeuke) by putting the open left hand against the base of right fist.	左拳槌で下段へ打ち込み、右拳は脇へ引く。 Execute Left-Kentsui toward Gedan (lower) and pull back the right fist to the side of body.	右下段払い、左拳は脇へ引く。 Execute Right-Gedanbarai with right fist and pull back left fist to left side of body.
留意点 Point				最短距離で左拳打込みが極ったら、直ぐに左足を引いて四股立ち、右下段払いを行う。左拳・右拳の大振り・腰の上下は不可。 Immediately after finishing straight Ken-Uchi with left fist, Shikodachi by pulling back left foot and execute Right-Gedanbarai. Don't overswing right and left fist and also don't move up and down of the hips.
分解 Kumite in detail			中段突きをしてくるのを、前足を引いて左小手で受ける。 When opponent comes back with Chudantsuki, withdraw front foot and block with left Kote.	腕を捕って引き寄せ、右肘当て。 Grabbing his right arm with blocking left hand and pulling him together, strike toward his Chudan with right elbow.

162　セイエンチン　SEIENCHIN

27 挙動	28 挙動	29 挙動
南東　Southeast	南東　Southeast	南東　Southeast

左三戦立ち。	四股立ち。	四股立ち。
Left-Sanchindachi	Shikodachi	Shikodachi
右足を軸にして左足で円を描くようにして南東方向へ左足を1歩運ぶ。	前（左）足を軸にして南東方向へ右足を1歩踏み出す。	右足を後方へ1歩引く。
Pivoting on the right foot, take left foot a step toward southeast as if drawing a circle.	Pivoting on the front (left) foot, take right foot one step toward southeast and lowe hips.	Pull right foot one step backward.
右手は開いて左拳槌部に添えて左中段外受けを行う（拳支え受け）。	右拳槌で下段へ打ち込み左拳は脇へ引く。	左下段払い、右拳は脇へ引く。
Execute Chudan-Sotouke (Ken-Sasaeuke) by putting the open right hand against the base of left fist.	Strike toward lower by right Kentsui, pull back left fist to side of the body.	Execute Left-Gedanbarai with left fist and pull back right fist to right side of the body.

写真㉝〜㊴の分解　　SEIENCHIN Kumite in detail

中段突きを、右中段拳支え受け。

Block opponent's Right-Chudantsuki with Right-Chudan-Ken-Sasaeuke, while drawing front foot toward left diagonally.

手首を捕ると同時に、四股立ちとなり、左拳槌で急所に当てる。

While taking his right wrist with right hand, step left foot in to become Shikodachi, then, strike his groin with Left-Kentsui.

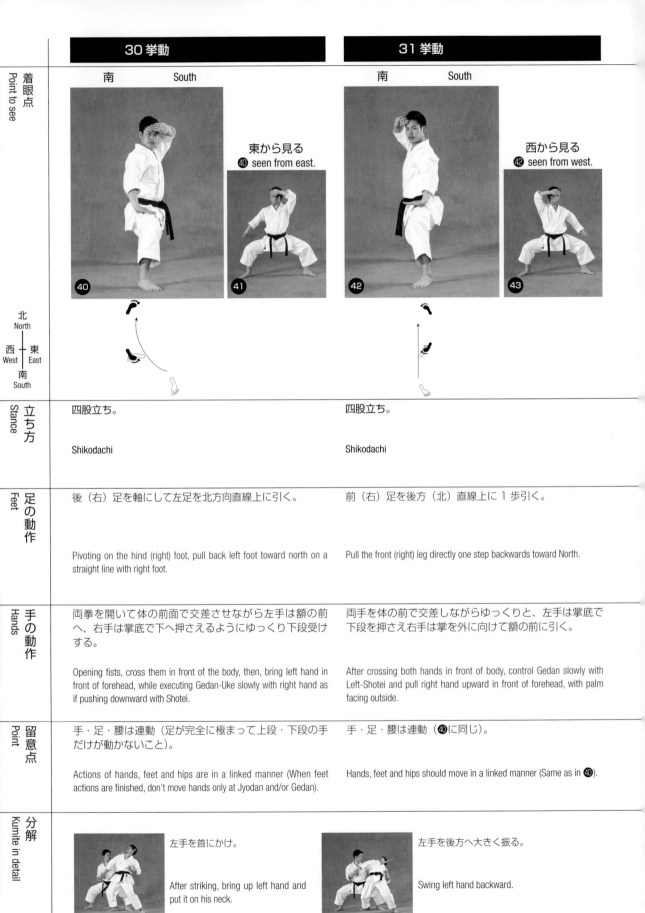

32 挙動

南　South

東から見る
㊹ seen from east.

右基立ち。

Right-Motodachi

右足を前（南）へ1歩踏み出す。

Take right foot one step forward (toward south).

左手は開いて体の前へ出し、右内受けを左掌に当てる。

Put left hand open in front of the body, hit it against Right-Uchiuke.

相手を後方へ倒す。

Take the opponent down backwards.

33 挙動

南　South

㊻から直ちに肩の高さに引く。

From ㊻ pull back Uraken to the shoulder height.

右基立ち。

Right-Motodachi

前へ寄り足にて進む。

Step forward with drag (Yoriashi).

右裏拳にて上段を打つ。

Hit toward Jyodan with Right-Uraken, and pull back toward shoulder height immediately.

突く。

Lower hips and finish with Tsuki.

34 挙動

	南　　　South	北東　　　Northeast	
着眼点 Point to see	 ㊽ 途中	 ㊾	 北東から見る ㊾ seen from northeast. ㊿
立ち方 Stance	左三戦立ちになる途中。 On the way to Left-Sanchindachi	左三戦立ち。 Left-Sanchindachi	
足の動作 Feet	前足（右）を左足前に移動する。 Bring front (right) foot in front of left foot.	体を北東へ回す。 Turn body toward northeast.	
手の動作 Hands	㊼のまま。 Same as in ㊼.	左中段外受け、右手は体の下方（正中線）へ伸ばして構える。 While executing Left-Chudan-Sotouke with left fist, stretch right hand toward lower part of body and hold there (Seichusen).	
留意点 Point			

方位図: 北 North / 西 West / 東 East / 南 South

分解 Kumite in detail

写真㊵～㊷の分解　SEIENCHIN Kumite in detail

中段蹴りを、右手で掬いあげて捕る。

When opponent attacks with Chudangeri, grad his right foot with right hand as if scooping.

上段突きを揚げ受けし、腕を捕り。

When he attacks further with Jyodantsuki, grad his right wrist with left hand.

35 挙動	36 挙動
北東　Northeast	北東　Northeast
  北東から見る ㊿ seen from northeast.	  北西から見る ㊼ seen from northwest.
左三戦立ち。	四股立ち。
Left-Sanchindachi	Shikodachi
㊾のまま。	右足を北東へ1歩運ぶ。
Same as in ㊾.	Take right foot one step toward northeast.
左手を開いて掌を前に向けて掛け手をする。	右拳で上段揚突き、左手は開いて手首を立て水月前に構える。
Open left hand and execute Kakete, with palm facing forward.	Execute Right-Jodan-Agetsuki, and position open left hand in front of solar plexus, bending wrist so the fingers face upright.
左中段外受けから左掛け手に移るとき左手は上下動させないこと。	【備考】揚突きは相手の顎（あご）のあたりに当てる。揚突きした拳は直ちに肩の高さに引く。
Don't move left hand up and down while executing from Left-Chudan-Sotouke to Left-Kakete.	<Note>Agetsuki should his around opponent's jaw. After Agetsuki, fist should be pulled back to shoulder height immediately.

左足で金的を蹴る。

Finish by kicking Kinteki (groin) with left foot.

写真㊹〜㊻の分解　　SEIENCHIN Kumite in detail

中段突きをしてくるのを、前足を後方へ引くと同時に、右中段内受け。

Hitting opponent's Chudantsuki sideways with Right-Chudan-Uchiuke, while withdrawing front foot.

	37 挙動	38 挙動
着眼点 / Point to see	北東 Northeast ⑤⑤ 裏打ちを引いたときを南東から見る ㊄ seen from southeast. ⑤⑥ 裏打ちした拳は直ちに肩の高さに引く。 Pull back the fist of Urauchi to the shoulder height.	北東 Northeast ⑤⑦
立ち方 / Stance	四股立ち。 Shikodachi	四股立ち。 Shikodachi
足の動作 / Feet	㊵のまま。 Same as in ㊵.	㊵のまま。 Same as in ㊵.
手の動作 / Hands	右上段裏打ち。 Hit Right-Jyodan-Urauchi.	右手で下段払いをする。水月前の左手は脇へ引く。 Execute Right-Gedanbarai. Pull back left hand in front of solar plexus to the left side of the body.
留意点 / Point	揚突きから上段裏打ち・下段払いの時上体が前後に振れないこと。 While executing from Agetsuki to Jyodan-Urauchi and Gedanbarai, don't move up and down of upper body.	
分解 / Kumite in detail	ただちに右拳で顔面へ裏打ちする。 Counter with Right-Urauchi to his face.	写真㊾〜㊽・㊿〜㊽の分解　SEIENCHIN Kumite in detail 中段突きを、左中段外受け。 Block opponent's Right-Chudantsuki with Left-Chudan-Sotouke, while withdrawing front foot.

168　セイエンチン　SEIENCHIN

39 挙動	40 挙動
北東　　Northeast	南　　South

東から見る
59 seen from east.

四股立ち。	右猫足立ち。
Shikodachi	Right-Nekoashidachi
右足を南西へ引く。	右足を左足の前に引き、踵をあげる。
Pull back right foot toward southwest.	Pull right foot in front of left foot, and raise heel.
左下段払いを行い、右拳は脇へ引く。	両手の肘を前後に引くようにして、右肘は腕を肩の高さにあげ、左肘は後方へ当てる。
Execute Left-Gedanbarai. Pull back right fist to right side of body.	Pulling both elbows apart from each other, lift right elbow up to shoulder height and push left elbow backward.
	前の肘はハズシ技であるからコースに留意（当ての動作にならないこと）。 【備考】普通の猫足立ちよりやや腰を落とし、尻を後ろへ出すようにする。 Front elbow is an evading technique and its moving route should be done carefully (Don't take hitting action). <Note>Hips are lower than usual Nekoashidachi and push buttocks slightly backward.

相手の手首を捕り、

After Chudan-Uke, turn around left wrist to grab his right wrist.

四股立ちになり右手を下に引きつけ、同時に右拳で顎（あご）に揚げ突きする。

While pulling his right hand downward at Shikodachi, execute Agetsuki to his jaw with right fist.

	41 挙動	42 挙動	
Point to see 着眼点	南 South 	南 South 途中 	北西 Northwest 
Stance 立ち方	左猫足立ち。 Left-Nekoashidachi	右三戦立ちになる途中。 On the way to Right-Sanchindachi.	右三戦立ち。 Right-Sanchindachi
Feet 足の動作	右足を後ろ（北）へ引き、左足はすこし引いて踵をあげる。 Pull right foot backward (toward north) and lift left heel up, after pulling back left foot slightly.	前足（左）を右足前に移動する。 Bring front (left) foot toward inside and in front of right foot.	体を北西に向ける。 Turn body toward northwest.
Hands 手の動作	左腕は肘を前にして肩の高さにあげ、右肘は後方へ当てる。 While lifting left arm until elbow comes to shoulder height and facing forward, execute right elbow attack backward with right arm.	⑥のまま。 Same as in ⑥.	右手は中段外受けを行い、左手は伸ばして体の下方（正中線）に構える。 While executing Right-Chudan-Sotouke, stretch left hand toward lower part of the body and hold there.
Point 留意点			
Kumite in detail 分解	 右拳で顔面に裏打ちする。 After Agetsuki, execute Urauchi to his face with right fist.	 相手がさらに中段突きしてくるのを、右拳で下段払い。 Block his further Chudantsuki with Right-Gedanbarai by hitting his left hand sideways.	

43 挙動	44 挙動	45 挙動
北西　Northwest	北西　Northwest	北西　Northwest

右三戦立ち。	四股立ち。	四股立ち。
Right-Sanchindachi	Shikodachi	Shikodachi
❻❸のまま。	左足を北西へ1歩進め、腰を落とす。	❻❺のまま。
Same as in ❻❸.	Take left foot a step toward northwest and lower hips.	Same as in ❻❺.
中段受けした右手を開き、掌を前に向けて掛け手をする。	左拳で上段揚突きを行い、右手は開いて手首を立て、水月前に構える。	左上段裏打ちを行う。裏打ちした拳は直ちに肩の高さに引く。
Opening right hand after finishing Chudan-Uke, execute Kakete, with palm facing forward.	Execute Jyodan-Agetsuki with left fist, while bending wrist upward, hold right hand in front of abdomen, with palm facing forward.	Execute Left-Jyodan-Urauchi. Pull back the fist of Urauchi to the shoulder height.

続いてくる中段蹴りを、前足を右斜め後方へ引き左手で下段払い。

Block his further Left-Chudangeri with Left-Gedanbarai, while withdrawing front foot.

右中段突きで極める。

Finish with Right-Chudantsuki.

	46 挙動	47 挙動	48 挙動
着眼点 Point to see	北西 Northwest	北西 Northwest	南 South

立ち方 Stance	四股立ち。 Shikodachi	四股立ち。 Shikodachi	左猫足立ち。 Left-Nekoashidachi
足の動作 Feet	(65)のまま。 Same as in (65).	右足を軸にして左足を後方（南東）へ引く。 Pivoting on the right foot pull left foot backward (toward southeast).	左足を右足前に引き、踵をあげる。 Pull back left foot in front of right foot, and raise heel.
手の動作 Hands	左下段払い。右拳は脇へ引く。 Execute Left-Gedanbarai with left fist. Pull back right fist to right side of the body.	右下段払い。左拳は脇へ引く。 Execute Right-Gedanbarai with right fist. Pull back left fist to left side of the body.	左手は肘を前にして肩の高さにあげ、右手は後方へ肘当てをする。 While lifting left arm until elbow is shoulder height and facing forward, execute elbow attack backward with right arm.
留意点 Point			

分解 Kumite in detail

写真(59)、(61)・(69)、(70)の分解 *SEIENCHIN Kumite in detail*

後方より相手に組みつかれる。

Being held from behind.

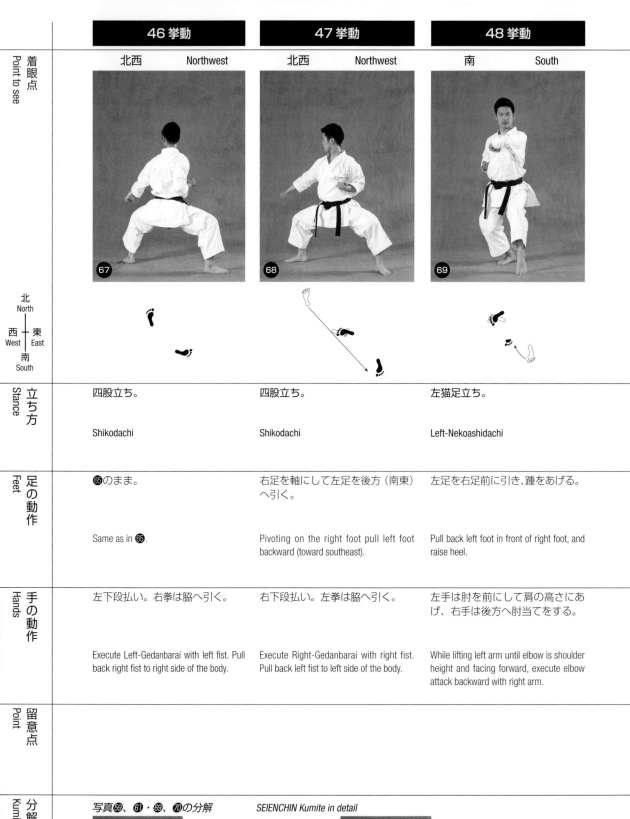

猫足立ちのように腰を落とし、尻を後ろへ出し、右腕は肩の高さにあげて相手の腕をはずし、左肘当て。

Lowering hips and pushing buttocks backward like Nekoashidachi, lift right arm until shoulder height to unlock opponent's arm and hit backward with left elbow.

49 挙動	50 挙動
南　South	南　South

東から見る
㉛ seen from east.

右猫足立ち。	右猫足立ち。
Right-Nekoashidachi	Right-Nekoashidachi
左足を後方（北）へ引き、右足は少し引いて踵をあげる。	⑳のまま。
Pull left foot backward (toward north) and draw back right foot a little and lift right heel.	Same as in ⑳.
右腕は肘を前にして肩の高さにあげ、左肘で後方へ当てる。	左手を開いて手首を立てて右手の上より掌底にて中段を押さえる。
While lifting right arm until elbow comes to shoulder height and facing forward, execute elbow attack backward with left arm.	Open left hand and bend wrist upward on top of the right fist, then, press Chudan with Shotei.

後方へ向き中段突き。

Turn around immediately and finish with Right-Chudantsuki.

51 挙動

	南　South	南　South
着眼点 Point to see	 　東から見る　⑬ seen from east.	 途中　　東から見る　⑮ seen from east.

北 North　西 West　東 East　南 South

立ち方 Stance	右猫足立ち。 Right-Nekoashidachi	猫足立ちになる途中。 On the way to stand Nekoashidachi.
足の動作 Feet	猫足立ちのまま前足（踵から）から波足で前に進む。 With the same Nekoashidachi stance, step forward with drag (Namiashi), from front foot first.	右足を後方（北）へ引く。 Pull right foot backward (toward north).
手の動作 Hands	波足で進みながら上段に右拳で裏打ちをし、直ちに肩の高さへ引く。 While stepping with drag (Namiashi), execute Urauchi toward Jyodan with right first, then, pull back it to shoulder height immediately.	裏打ちの状態から右手を引いて両肘を合わせるようにし。 Pull both hands toward face and put both elbows together.
留意点 Point	左掌底は押さえた所から動かないこと。 Don't move from where Left-Shotei is executed.	
分解 Kumite in detail	　写真⑪～⑰の分解　**SEIENCHIN Kumite in detail** 中段突きを、猫足立ち左手掌底にて下に押さえ。 To counter opponent's Right-Chudantsuki, withdraw front foot to become Nekoashidachi and, at the same time, pressing downward with Left-Shotei.	右拳にて顔面へ裏打ち。 Execute Urauchi to his face with right fist.

セイエンチン　SEIENCHIN

52 挙動		止め
南　South	南　South	南　South
	途中 	
⑦	⑧	⑨
左猫足立ち。	結び立ち。	結び立ち。
Left-Nekoashidachi	Musubidachi	Musubidachi
ひき続き左足を引き寄せる。	左足を右足に引きつける。	⑱のまま。
Continue to pull pack left foot.	Pull left foot to the right foot.	Same as in ⑱.
両肘を体の前で合わせ、さらに両肘を左右に張る。両掌は合わせ山型となる（肘繰り受け）。	両手は開き、左掌に右甲を重ね、腹部前に上げる。	両手を返し、下を押すように構える。
Face both elbows in front of the body and spread both elbows to both sides of body, and tips of hands touching, from a "mountain" with palms (Hijikuri-Uke).	Open both hands, placing the back of the right hand on top of the palm of the left, and raise up to in front of the abdomen.	Revolve both hands inward then, as if pushing downward, move into position.
両肘は繰り受けのコースを通すこと。 【備考】⑱の右裏打ちから、右足を引いて左猫足立ち、肘繰り受けの動作は連動のこと。 "Both elbows should follow the form of Kuriuke. < Note > the movements following Urauchi in ⑱ ,pulling back the right leg into left Nekoashidachi and executing Hijikuri-Uke, should be linked."		

空いた脇へさらに中段突きをしてくるのを、内側より肘を入れて受ける。
Block his further Left-Chudantsuki to the open side of body with right elbow from inside (Hijikuri-Uke).

腰を落として四股立ちとなり、脇を肘当てで極める。
Lower hips to become Shikodachi and finish with right elbow attack to his left side of body.

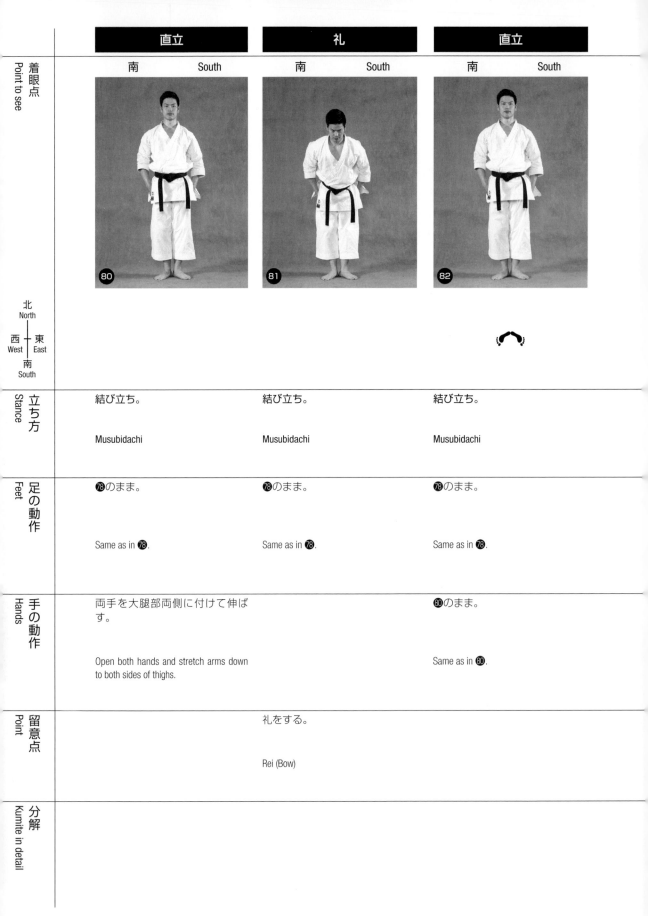

セイシャン
SEISHAN

特徴
前半は全身の力を均等に使って技が止ることなくリズミカルに動作する。
後半は前半の応用動作で立ち方に特徴がある。

Specialty
In first half of SEISHAN edition, movements should be done rhythmically without stopping of waza in applying strength of whole body equally. Last half of this edition explains practical movements in application of first half edition with particular stance (tachikata).

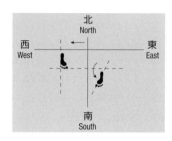

横セイシャンの立ち方
①左右の足幅はナイハンチ立ち程度
②前足先を内輪にし、後ろ足はごくわずかに内輪にする。体をすこし沈め、膝は柔らかにする。
③両足の前後の距離は、前足踵の後側と後足指先とが、一直線上より少し離れる。

Stance of YOKO-SEISHAN
①Width between feet should be almost same as that of Naihanchidachi (standing naturally).
②Front foot points inward and also turns hind foot slightly inward. Lower body slightly and loosen knee joints.
③The Distance between the tip of the rear foot and the heel of the front foot should be slightly more apart than horizontal to each other.

横セイシャンの進み方
①（左足前の場合）左足踵をすこし内転し、右足を内輪にしながら、内側から外側に幾分弧を描くように前に進め、前記の立ち方になる。
②体の重心をはずさず、上体を正面向きのまま、右足全体を柔らかに運ぶ。

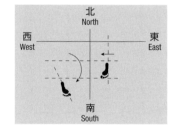

Feet of YOKO-SEISHAN
①(left foot in front) Turn left foot's heel slightly inward and, while turning right foot inward, advance it such like drawing a circle form inside to outside.
②Putting body gravity in between both feet with upper body facing front, advance right leg softly.

縦セイシャンの立ち方
①左右の足幅を少なくし、後足踵の内側縁と、前足拇指先縁が同一線上にあるように内輪にする。
②前後の足幅は、（横）セイシャン立ちをそのまま縦にした足幅程度となる。

Stance of TATE-SEISHAN
①Reduce width between both feet, inside of hind heel and tip of front foot's big toe (facing inward) should be on the same line.
②Width between foot should be same as that of Seishandachi.

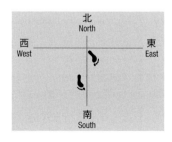

179

	直立	礼	直立
着眼点 Point to see	南　　　South	南　　　South	南　　　South
	❶	❷	❸

北 North
西 West ― 東 East
南 South

	直立	礼	直立
立ち方 Stance	結び立ち。 Musubidachi	結び立ち。 Musubidachi	結び立ち。 Musubidachi
足の動作 Feet	結び立ち。 Musubidachi	❶のまま。 Same as in ❶.	❶のまま。 Same as in ❶.
手の動作 Hands	両手は開いて、大腿部前に軽く添える。 Open both hands and place them in front of thighs.		❶のまま。 Same as in ❶.
留意点 Point		礼をする。 Rei (Bow)	
分解 Kumite in detail			

180　セイシャン　SEISHAN

用意

南　　　South	南　　　South	南　　　South
	途中	途中
❹	❺	❻

 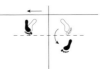

八字立ち。	左横セイシャン立ち（左足踵の後側の横一線より、右足先が少し離れる程度に立つ）。	左横セイシャン立ち
Hachijidachi	Left-Yoko-Seishandachi (tip of right foot's big toe should be slightly in front of the line of back of left heel).	Left-Yoko-Seishandachi
結び立ちから足を左、右と開き、八字立ちとなる（両踵の間隔は1足長半）。	右踵をやや外転し、左足を内輪にし、内側より弧を描きながら南に進める。	❺のまま。
Open left foot and then right foot (width of heels is a foot and half apart) to stand Hachijidachi.	Turn right foot's heel outward a little while turning left foot inward, advance it to south as if drawing a circle from inside.	Same as in ❺.
両手は大腿部前で軽く握る。	両拳を胸前で交差（右腕上）しながら、足が極まると同時に満身の力を入れて動作に入る。	
Grip both hands lightly in front of thighs.	While crossing both arms (right arm on top) in front of the chest, start movement with whole strength of body as soon as feet are fixed.	

	1 挙動	2 挙動	
着眼点 Point to see	南　South	南　South	南　South
	⑦⑧ 西から見る ⑦ seen from west.	⑨	途中 ⑩
	北 North 西 West ｜ 東 East 南 South		
立ち方 Stance	左横セイシャン立ち Left-Yoko-Seishandachi	左横セイシャン立ち Left-Yoko-Seishandachi	右横セイシャン立ち。 Right-Yoko-Seishandachi
足の動作 Feet	❺のまま。 Same as in ❺.	❺のまま。 Same as in ❺.	左踵をやや内転し、右足を内側より弧を描きながら南に進める。 While turning left heel slightly inward, advance right foot toward south as if drawing a circle from inside.
手の動作 Hands	左中段外受け（下位）をする。右拳は体側（下位）に引く。 Left-Chudan-Sotouke (lower position). Pull back right fist to right side of body.	右拳中段突き（下位）をする。左拳は体側（下位）に引く。 Right-Chudantsuki (lower position). Pull back left fist to left side of body.	右拳を左下腹前に運ぶ。 Move the right fist to in front of the left side of the lower abdomen.
留意点 Point	1〜16の挙動は、全身均等に満身の力で、柔らかになめらかに緩やかに動作する。脇の締めが緩み、肘が体より離れて上下に動くことと、反対の引き手が不十分にならないこと。 Motion 1-16 must be done with all strength spreading over whole body evenly and with smooth and quiet movement. Take care neither loosen underarm, nor to move elbows up and down apart from the body, nor to be incomplete of pulling the hands.		【備考】足の運びは「横セイシャン」の進み方を参照。以下同じ。 <Note>As for feet movements refer to "Feet of Yoko-Seishan".
分解 Kumite in detail			

182　セイシャン　SEISHAN

	3 挙動	4 挙動
南　　　South	南　　　South	南　　　South
途中		
 ⑪	 ⑫	 ⑬

右横セイシャン立ち。	右横セイシャン立ち。	右横セイシャン立ち。
Right-Yoko-Seishandachi	Right-Yoko-Seishandachi	Right-Yoko-Seishandachi
⑩のまま。	⑩のまま。	⑩のまま。
Same as in ⑩.	Same as in ⑩.	Same as in ⑩.
右前腕を返しながら。	右中段外受け（下位）をする。左拳は体側に引いたまま。	左拳中段突き（下位）をする。右拳は体側（下位）に引く。
Rotate the right fist out back towards the right.	Right-Chudan-Sotouke (lower position). Left fist remains the same.	Left-Chudantsuki (lower position). Pull back right fist to right side of the body.
移動のとき前足の爪先が外に向かないように。	【備考】1 挙動❼の左右反対の形。	【備考】2 挙動❾の左右反対動作。
In movement, pay attention not to turn front foot toe outside.	<Note>Reverse of ❼.	<Note>Reverse of ❾.

183

		5 挙動	6 挙動	
着眼点 Point to see		南　　　　South 	南　　　　South 	南　　　　South 途中
		北 North 西┼東 West East 南 South		
立ち方 Stance		左横セイシャン立ち。 Left-Yoko-Seishandachi	左横セイシャン立ち。 Left-Yoko-Seishandachi	左横セイシャン立ち。 Left-Yoko-Seishandachi
足の動作 Feet		左足を南に進め、1挙動の立ち方となる。 Advance left foot toward south.	⓮のまま。 Same as in ⓮.	⓮のまま。 Same as in ⓮.
手の動作 Hands		左中段外受け（下位）をする。右拳は引いたまま。 Left-Chudan-Sotouke (lower position). Right fist remains the same.	右拳中段突き（下位）をする。左拳は体側（下位）に引く。 Right-Chudantsuki (lower position). Pull back left fist to left side of the body.	両拳を人差指一本拳（コーサー）にする。（両拳先は軽く触れる程度）。 Both hands execute Hitosashiyubi (forefinger) Ipponken (Kousa, with the middle knuckle). The tips of the Ipponken knuckles should be touching very slightly.
留意点 Point		【備考】3挙動⓬の左右反対動作。 <Note>Same as in ⓬ (left and right is riversed).	【備考】4挙動⓭の左右反対動作。 <Note>Same as in ⓭ (left and right is riversed).	
分解 Kumite in detail				

184　セイシャン　SEISHAN

7 挙動		8 挙動
南 South	南 South	南 South
 ⑰	 途中 ⑱	 ⑲
左横セイシャン立ち。	左横セイシャン立ち。	左横セイシャン立ち。
Left-Yoko-Seishandachi	Left-Yoko-Seishandachi	Left-Yoko-Seishandachi
⑭のまま。	⑭のまま。	⑭のまま。
Same as in ⑭.	Same as in ⑭.	Same as in ⑭.
胸の中央部、乳のすこし上のところに運び、両肘を挙上する。		人差指一本拳（コーサー）のまま、左右同時に中段突き（下位）をする。
Lift both hands through the center of the torso to just above the chest, raising both elbows.		With Hitosashiyubi-Ipponken (Kousa), Chudantsuki (lower position) with both fists at the same time.
肘受けの基礎動作。肘上げは手首を曲げてはならない。		肘を絞り込みながら手首を曲げないで突き下す。
Basic motion of Hijiuke. Don't bend wrists at Hijiage.		Squeezing both elbows, Tsukioroshi without bending wrists.

写真⑰の分解　　SEISHAN Kumite in detail

		9 挙動	

	南　　　South	南　　　South	南　　　South

着眼点
Point to see

	途中		途中
	⑳	㉑	㉒

北
North

西 — 東
West｜East

南
South

立ち方 / Stance

左横セイシャン立ち。	左横セイシャン立ち。	左横セイシャン立ち。
Left-Yoko-Seishandachi	Left-Yoko-Seishandachi	Left-Yoko-Seishandachi

足の動作 / Feet

⓮のまま。	⓮のまま。	⓮のまま。
Same as in ⓮.	Same as in ⓮.	Same as in ⓮.

手の動作 / Hands

両手を手刀にする。	前方より、両前膊橈骨側で上段払い受けを両側方に左右同時に行う（両掌面は向き合う）。	
Both hands open into Shuto.	Moving up from the front, raise both forearms into Jodan-Haraiuke. Be sure to move both sides simultaneously. The palms of the hands face each other.	

留意点 / Point

		肘を少し押し出しながら力点を手首の方に移し切り下げる。肘が止まって手首の方が先に動かないように。
		Pushing out both elbows a little, move power point toward wrists. Wrists must not move while elbows are left unmoved.

分解 / Kumite in detail

写真㉑〜㉓の分解　　　*SEISHAN Kumite in detail*

186　　セイシャン　SEISHAN

10 挙動

| 南 South | 南 South | 途中 | 途中 |

㉓

㉔

㉕

左横セイシャン立ち。	右足を前に両脚を交差する。	
Left-Yoko-Seishandachi	Cross both legs with right foot in front.	
⓯のまま。	左足を軸とし、右足を千鳥に交差し南東に運ぶ。	
Same as in ⓯.	Pivoting on the left foot, step right foot toward southeast.	
両手刀の前膊尺骨側で、押し下げるように両側方に同時に下段手刀払いをする。	両手刀は胸前で交差し（右掌面下向きで下側、左掌面上向きで上側）。	
Gedanbarai with ulna parts of both Shuto at the same time as if pushing downward to both side of the body.	Cross both arms in front of chest with left hand (palm facing upward) on top of right hand (palm facing downward).	
		膝を柔らかく使い、重心移動を正確に行う。腰が曲がったり、中心軸が大きくぶれたりしないこと。
		Using both knees flexibly, gravity movement should be done precisely. Waist must not bend or central axis of the body must not move a lot.

11 挙動

着眼点 Point to see	 北 Nortth	 ㉕から㉖までの動作を北から見る ㉕ to ㉖ seen from north.  東から見る ㉖ seen from east. 
北 North 西 West ― 東 East 南 South		
立ち方 Stance	左横セイシャン立ち。 Left-Yoko-Seishandachi	
足の動作 Feet	体を左に回転させ、両足先は北に向く。 Turn body to left and both toes point north.	
手の動作 Hands	左手刀下段払い。右手刀は掌面上向きに撓骨側で中段外受けをする（右手首をわずかに背屈する）。 Gedanbarai with Left-Shuto. Right-Shuto is palm upwards, and executes Chudan-Sotouke with forearm (the wrist is slightly bent downward).	
留意点 Point	中段、下段の受けを同時に行う。下段の肘が体側外に出るのは肘が浮き受けが弱くなる。 Execute Chudan-Uke and Gedan-Uke at the same time. In case Gedan elbow comes out of the body, the elbow loosens and weakens defense.	
分解 Kumite in detail	写真㉖〜㉛の分解　SEISHAN Kumite in detail 	①、②、③の手の動きをクローズアップしてみる。  右腕を後方に引きつつ、手首を十分背屈しながら手掌を返し、 Pulling right arm backward, turn around palm with wrist bending backward.

188　セイシャン　SEISHAN

12 挙動

北　　　North

北から見る　東から見る
㉛ seen from north.　㉛ seen from east.

北　　　North

途中

左横セイシャン立ち。	右横セイシャン立ち。
Left-Yoko-Sheishandachi	Right-Yoko-Sheishandachi
㉖のまま。	右足を北に進める。
Same as in ㉖.	Advance right foot toward north.
右腕を後方に引きつつ、手首を背屈させたまま掌面を返し、右手を体側下方に引く。左手はそのまま。	両手刀は胸前で交差し（左掌面下向きで下側、右掌面上向きで上側）。
Slowly pulling the right arm back, with the wrist still bent turn the palm over and pull to the lower right side of the waist. Do not move left hand.	Cross both arms in front of chest with right hand (palm facing upward) on top of left hand (palm facing downward).
手首をわずかに撓骨側に背屈し、相手の突きを払い受けて懸ける気持ち。懸け手は体側より、離さず、手首のみ背屈させながら背手、手刀の順で斜め下後方に引く。Twist right wrist outward as if hooking opponent's Tsuki with Haraiuke. Pull back right arm diagonally in the order of Haishu and Shuto, twisting wrist only outside without parting from body.	【備考】㉗の左右反対の形。 <Note>Right and left side is reversed with ㉗.

Close-up of ①,② and ③

右手刀の掌面が平らになる程度に手首を背屈し、さらに撓骨側にわずかに外屈しながら、払い受けをする。
Bend wrist backward so that palm of Right-Shuto becomes horizontal. Then turning it slightly outward toward radius side, execute Haraiuke.

相手の手首を親指と薬指、小指で握って引く（他の指は自然に添える）。
Grab and pull opponent's left wrist with thumb, ring finger and little finger (other fingers placed naturally).

	13 挙動	14 挙動	

	北　　　North	北　　　North	北　　　North
着眼点 Point to see	㉟	㊱	途中 ㊲

北
North
西━東
West┃East
南
South

立ち方 Stance	右横セイシャン立ち。 Right-Yoko-Sheishandachi	右横セイシャン立ち。 Right-Yoko-Seishandachi	左横セイシャン立ち。 Left-Yoko-Seishandachi
足の動作 Feet	㉞のまま。 Same as in ㉞ .	㉞のまま。 Same as in ㉞ .	左足を北に進める。 Advance left foot toward north.
手の動作 Hands	右手刀下段払い、左（手刀撓骨側）中段外受けをする。 Gedanbarai with Right-Shuto. Chudan-Sotouke with radius side of Left-Shuto.	左手掌を返しながら体側下方に引く。右手そのまま。 While turning around left palm, pull back left hand to left side of body. Right hand remains same.	両手刀は胸前で交差し（右掌面下向きで下側、左掌面上向きで上側）。 Cross both arms in front of chest with left hand (palm facing upward) on top of right hand (palm facing downward).
留意点 Point	【備考】㉖の左右反対の形。 <Note>Right and left side is reversed with ㉖.	【備考】㉛の左右反対の形。 <Note>Right and left side is reversed with ㉛.	【備考】㉗に同じ。 <Note>Same as in ㉗.
分解 Kumite in detail			

190　セイシャン　SEISHAN

15 挙動	16 挙動	17 挙動
北　　　　North	北　　　　North	東　　　　East

左横セイシャン立ち。	左横セイシャン立ち。	右縦セイシャン立ち（右足拇指先と左踵の内側が同一線上になる）。
Left-Yoko-Seishandachi	Left-Yoko-Seishandachi	Right-Tate-Seishandachi (tip of right foot's big toe should be on the line of inside of left heel).
㊲のまま。	㊲のまま。	右足前で東に寄り足で進める。
Same as in ㊲.	Same as in ㊲.	Take right foot leaping step toward east. Left foot following in Yoriashi.
左手刀下段払い、右（手刀撓骨側）中段外受けをする。	右手掌を返しながら、体側下方に引く。左手そのまま。	右拳上段外受け、左拳は体側に引く。
Gedanbarai with Left-Shuto. Chudan-Sotouke with radius side of Right-Shuto.	While turning around right palm, pull back right hand to right side of body. Left hand remains the same.	Jyodan-Sotouke with right fist. Pull back left fist to left side of the body.
【備考】㉖に同じ。	【備考】㉛に同じ。	上段払い受けを腕の力だけで受けたり、前屈立ちにならないようにし、後ろ足の踵が浮いたり外側に流れて動いてはならない。
<Note>Same as in ㉖.	<Note>Same as in ㉛.	Don't defense only with arm strength, nor by Zenkutsudachi, nor with up left heel. Don't move left heel away outside.

サイファ　セーパイ　ジオン　カンクウダイ　バッサイダイ　セイエンチン　セイシャン　チントウ

		18挙動	19挙動
着眼点 Point to see	東　　East 途中 ㊶	東　　East ㊷	西　　West ㊸
	北 North 西━┿━東 West　East 南 South		
立ち方 Stance	右縦セイシャン立ち。 Right-Tate-Seishandachi	右縦セイシャン立ち。 Right-Tate-Seishandachi	左縦セイシャン立ち。 Left-Tate-Seishandachi
足の動作 Feet	㊵のまま。 Same as in ㊵ .	㊵のまま。 Same as in ㊵ .	体を180°左回りし、左足前で西に寄り足で進める。 Turn body 180° to left and take left foot leaping step toward west. Right foot follows in Yoriashi.
手の動作 Hands	左、右と連続中段突きをする。引き手はそれぞれ体側に引く。 Repeat Chudantsuki with left and then right fist. Pull back each Hikite to each side of the body.		左拳上段外受け、右拳は体側に引く。 Jyodan-Sotouke with left fist. Pull back right fist to right side of the body.
留意点 Point	【備考】17、18挙動は連続して行なう。 <Note>Motion of 17 and 18 should be a continuous movement.		
分解 Kumite in detail			

192　セイシャン　SEISHAN

	20 挙動	21 挙動
西　　　West	西　　　West	北　　　North

左縦セイシャン立ち。	左縦セイシャン立ち。	右縦セイシャン立ち。
Left-Tate-Seishandachi	Left-Tate-Seishandachi	Right-Tate-Sheishandachi
㊸のまま。	㊸のまま。	体を 90°右転し、右足前で北に寄り足で進める。
Same as in ㊸	Same as in ㊸	Turn body 90° to right, then take right foot leaping step (Yoriashi) toward north.
右、左と連続中段突きをする。引き手はそれぞれ体側に引く。		右拳上段外受け。左拳は体側に引く。
Repeat Chudantsuki with right and then left fist. Pull back each Hikite to each side of the body.		Jyodan-Sotouke with right fist. Pull back left fist to left side of the body.
【備考】19、20 挙動は連続して行う（17、18 挙動の左右反対となる）。		
<Note>Motion 19 and 20 should be a continuous movement (riverse of motion 17 and 18).		

22 挙動

		北　　North	北　　North	北　　North
着眼点 Point to see		途中 (47)	(48)	途中 (49)

北から見る
(49) seen from north.
(50)

| | 北　North
西　東
West　East
南　South | | | |

立ち方 Stance	右縦セイシャン立ち。 Right-Tate-Seishandachi	右縦セイシャン立ち。 Right-Tate-Seishandachi	右片足で立つ。 Stand on right foot.
足の動作 Feet	(46)のまま。 Same as in (46).	(46)のまま。 Same as in (46).	後方からの踏込みに対し、左足を引いてかわすと同時に、前方に対し前蹴りの姿勢をとる。 While lifting left knee to dodge Fumikomi from behind, take stance for Maegeri.
手の動作 Hands	左、右と連続中段突きをする。引き手はそれぞれ体側に引く。 Repeat Chudantsuki with left and then right fist. Pull back each Hikite to each side of the body.		前蹴りの姿勢をとると同時に、左裏拳で相手の鼻を掬い打ち、右拳は体側に引く。 While taking stance for Maegeri, scoop opponent's nose upward with Left-Uraken. Pull back right fist to right side of the body.
留意点 Point	【備考】21、22 挙動は連続して行う（17、18 挙動に同じ）。 <Note>Motion 21 and 22 should be done continuously, and same as in motion 17 and 18.		
分解 Kumite in detail			

194　セイシャン　SEISHAN

23挙動

南　South	南　South	南　South
途中  (51)	 (52)	途中  (53)
	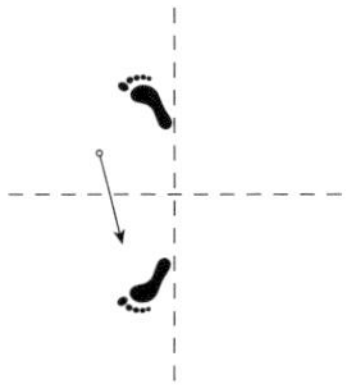	
右片足で立つ。 Stand on right foot.	四股立ち。 Shikodachi	右足を前に両脚を交差して立つ。 Stand with feet crossed with rightfoot in front.
体を左に回転させ、足先は北西を向く。 Turn body to left, tips pointing toward northwest.	左足を南に踏み込む。 Step in left foot toward south.	右足を左足の前に千鳥に交差させて、南に踏み出す。 Step right foot toward south and cross with left foot in Chidori.
掬いあげた左拳をそのまま頭上に構えながら。 Hold scooped up left fist above head. Right fist remains the same.	左裏拳を上より下に打ちおろす。右拳は体側に構えたまま。 Strike Left-Uraken downward. Right fist remains the same.	両拳はそのままに、左腕を相手に掴まれ引かれるにまかせて体を送り。 Both fists remain the same. Step out close to opponent by force of grasping left arm and pulling by him.

掬い打ちをしたあと、惰性で後ろを振り向いてはならない。打ちあげた腕の力が抜けないまま踏み込み、裏打ちを行うと何れも弱くなり立ち方も不安定となる。

After executing Sukuiuchi, never turn around by force of mere habit. If Fumikomi and Urauchi are executed without removing arm strength both Fumikomi and Urauchi debilitate original strength and will be instable at Tachikata.

写真㊾～(52)の分解　　*SEISHAN Kumite in detail*

24 挙動

着眼点 Point to see	南　　South 途中  ㊺	南　　South  ㊻	西から見る ㊻ seen from west.  ㊼

北 North／西 West／東 East／南 South

立ち方 Stance	右片足で立つ。 Standing on right foot.	順突きの突込み立ち（左前屈立ち、T字形）。 Junzukinotukkomidatchi (Left Zenkutsudachi with the feet in a 'T' shape).
足の動作 Feet	左横蹴りをする。 Left-Yokogeri.	蹴った左足を突込みの足におろす。 Put down left foot to become Tsukikomiashi.
手の動作 Hands	左横蹴りと同時に、左拳を強く体側に引く。右拳はそのまま。 While executing Left-Yokogeri, pull back left fist forcefully to left side of the body. Right fist remains the same.	左拳で下段に突っ込む。右拳は構えたまま。 Thrust left fist toward Gedan. Right fist remains the same.
留意点 Point	体の移動は腰を曲げたり、上下に動かさない。左拳の引きと蹴りは同時に行うが、引足が不十分だと後ろ足の膝や腰が曲がり下段突きが弱くなる。 Waist must not bend nor move up and down in movement. Pulling back left fist and kick are executed at the same time. However, if pulling back foot is insufficient, back foot knee and waist wrill bend and Gedantsuki will weaken.	
分解 Kumite in detail	写真㊼〜㊽の分解　　*SEISHAN Kumite in detail*     	

セイシャン　SEISHAN

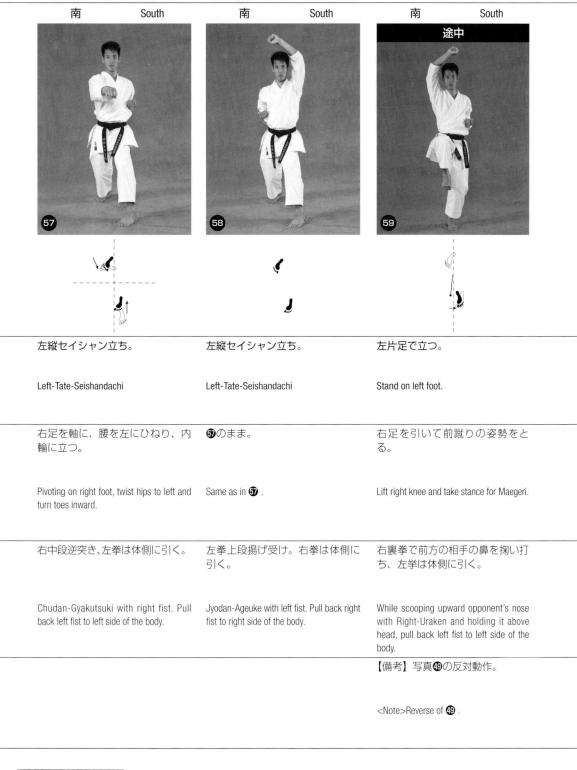

25 挙動 南 South	26 挙動 南 South	南 South 途中
左縦セイシャン立ち。	左縦セイシャン立ち。	左片足で立つ。
Left-Tate-Seishandachi	Left-Tate-Seishandachi	Stand on left foot.
右足を軸に、腰を左にひねり、内輪に立つ。	⑰のまま。	右足を引いて前蹴りの姿勢をとる。
Pivoting on right foot, twist hips to left and turn toes inward.	Same as in ⑰.	Lift right knee and take stance for Maegeri.
右中段逆突き、左拳は体側に引く。	左拳上段揚げ受け。右拳は体側に引く。	右裏拳で前方の相手の鼻を掬い打ち、左拳は体側に引く。
Chudan-Gyakutsuki with right fist. Pull back left fist to left side of the body.	Jyodan-Ageuke with left fist. Pull back right fist to right side of the body.	While scooping upward opponent's nose with Right-Uraken and holding it above head, pull back left fist to left side of the body.
		【備考】写真㊾の反対動作。
		<Note>Reverse of ㊾.

27 挙動

	北　North	北　North	北　North
着眼点 Point to see	途中 60	途中 61	途中 62
立ち方 Stance	左片足で立つ。 Stand on left foot.	四股立ち。 Shikodachi	左足を前に両脚を交差して立つ。 Feet crossed to stand with left foot in front.
足の動作 Feet	体を右に回転させ、足先は南西を向く。 Turn body to right, tips pointing toward southwest.	右足を北に踏み込む。 Step in right foot toward nouth.	左足を右足の前に千鳥に交差させ、北に踏み出す。 Step left foot toward north and cross with right foot in Chidori.
手の動作 Hands	掬いあげた右拳をそのまま頭上に構えながら。 Hold scooped up right fist above head. Left fist remains the same.	右裏拳を上より下に打ちおろす。左拳は体側に構えたまま。 Strike Right-Uraken downward. Left fist remains the same.	両拳はそのまま。 Both fists remains the same.
留意点 Point			【備考】24挙動を左右反対に行なう。 <Note>Reverse of motion 24.
分解 Kumite in detail			

198　セイシャン　SEISHAN

	28 挙動	29 挙動
北　　　North	北　　　North	北　　　North
途中		
63	64	65

左片足で立つ。	順突きの突込み立ち（右前屈立ち、T字形）。	右縦セイシャン立ち。
Standing on left foot.	Tsukikomiashi for Juntsuki (Right-Zenkutsudachi in T-shape).	Right-Tate Seishandachi.
右横蹴りをする。	蹴った右足を突込みの足におろす。	左足を軸に、腰を右にひねり内輪に立つ。
Right-Yokogeri.	Put down right foot to become Tsukikomiashi.	With left foot as axis, twist hips to right and turn toes inward.
右横蹴りと同時に、右拳を強く体側に引く。左拳はそのまま。	右拳で下段に突っ込む。左拳は構えたまま。	左中段逆突き、右拳は体側に引く。
While executing Right-Yokogeri, pull back right fist forcefully to right side of the body. Left fist remains the same.	Thrust right fist toward Gedan. Left fist remains the same.	Chudan-Gyakutsuki with left fist. Pull back right fist to right side of the body.
		下段の突込みから逆突（縦セイシャン立ち）になるが、そのとき腰を高くしてはならない。
		While movement proceeds from Tsukkomi of Gedan to Gyakutsuki (Tate-Seishandachi), never make waist position high.

サイファ　セーパイ　ジオン　カンクウダイ　バッサイダイ　セイエンチン　**セイシャン**　チントウ

30 挙動

	北 North	北 North（途中）	南 South（途中）
着眼点 Point to see	写真66	写真67	写真68
立ち方 Stance	右縦セイシャン立ち。 Right-Tate-Seishandachi	右片足で立つ。 Stand on right foot.	右片足で立つ。 Stand on right foot.
足の動作 Feet	65のまま。 Same as in 65.	左足を引いて前蹴りの姿勢をとる。 Lift left knee and take stance for Maegeri.	体を左に回転させ、足先は北西を向く。 Turn body to left, tips pointing toward northwest.
手の動作 Hands	右拳上段揚げ受け、左拳は体側に引く。 Jyodan-Ageuke with right fist. Pull back left fist to left side of the body.	左裏拳で上段に掬い打ち、右拳は体側に引く。 Execute Jyodan-Sukuiuchi with Left-Uraken, while pulling the right fist back to the right side of the body.	掬いあげた左拳をそのまま頭上に構えながら。 Hold scooped up left fist above head. Right fist remains the same.
留意点 Point		【備考】23挙動に同じ。 <Note>Same as in 23.	

分解 Kumite in detail

写真69〜71の分解　　SEISHAN Kumite in detail

200　セイシャン　SEISHAN

31 挙動		32 挙動
南　　　　South	南　　　　South	南　　　　South
	途中	
⑥⑨	⑦⓪	⑦①

四股立ち。	左片足で立つ。	左縦セイシャン立ち。
Shikodachi	Stand on left foot.	Left-Tate Seishandachi
左足を南に踏み込む。	左足を軸に、左掌に、右足で弧状蹴り（三日月蹴り）をなす（左手を掴んだ相手の手を蹴り払う）。	蹴った右足を北に引き、内輪に立つ。
Step in left foot toward south.	Kojyogeri (Mikazukigeri) against left palm with right foot (kick away opponent's hand grabbing your left hand).	Pull down right foot backward to north and turn toes inward.
左裏拳を上より下に打ちおろす。右拳は体側に構えたまま。	左手は開き、右蹴り足をあてる。右拳は体側に引いたまま。	右中段逆突き、左拳は体側に引く。
Strike Left-Uraken downward. Right fist remains the same.	Open left hand and kick against left palm with right foot. Right fist remains the same.	Chudan-Gyakutsuki with right fist. Pull back left fist to left side of body.
	三日月蹴りは腰の回転で行う。足だけ回して左手を下げて当ててはならない。	
	Mikazukigeri is performed by waist turn. Hitting by turning foot only with hanging down left hand should not be done.	

サイファ　セーパイ　ジオン　カンクウダイ　バッサイダイ　セイエンチン　**セイシャン**　チントウ

		33 挙動	止め

	南　South	南　South	南　South
着眼点 Point to see	途中 72	73	74

北 North
西 West ┼ 東 East
南 South

立ち方 Stance	右足はそのままに、左足爪先立ちで引きつける。 Staying right foot the same, pull left foot in tiptoeing.	左足爪先立ち。 Left- Tsumasakidachi.	八字立ち。 Hachijidachi
足の動作 Feet	左足を爪先立ちにして右足前に引きつけ、腰をやや右にひねって下半身をかばう。 Pull left foot in front of right into Tsumasakidachi. Keeping tight, twist hips slightly to the right to protect the lower half of the body.	72のまま。 Same as in 72.	右足を軸に、左足を引いて用意の姿勢にもどる。 Pivoting on right foot, pull back left foot and return to Yo-i posture.
手の動作 Hands	両手を猫手（五指を十分内屈させる）にして、両手首を背屈させて両体側に引きながら。 Both hands become Nekote (bend all fingers as much as possible inside of palms). Bend both wrists backward and pull back hands under both armpits.	体をやや落すと同時に両掌底を突きおろして、下段受けをする（両手首の内側が接する）。 While lowering body slightly, execute Gedanuke by thrusting both Shotei downward (both wrists touching on inside).	両手をそれぞれ大腿部前におろす。 Lower both hands in front of thighs.
留意点 Point		掌底受けはゆっくり行わない。引きつけた左足は膝を締め爪先を内に踵を外にする様に立つ。 Don't execute Shoteiuke slowly. Draw left foot to tight knee and stand with turning toe tips inside and heel outside.	止め、直れの場合も残心に注意する。 Pay attention on Zanshin (a state of alertness) at Yame and Naore.
分解 Kumite in detail	写真72〜73の分解　　SEISHAN Kumite in detail		

202　セイシャン　SEISHAN

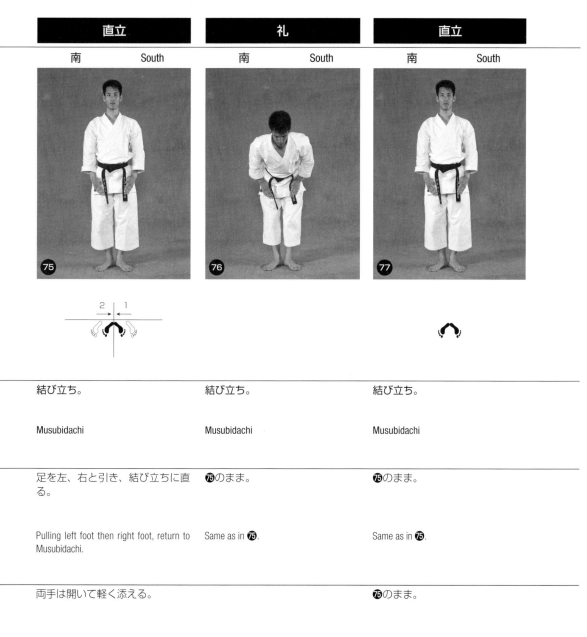

直立	礼	直立
南 South	南 South	南 South
結び立ち。	結び立ち。	結び立ち。
Musubidachi	Musubidachi	Musubidachi
足を左、右と引き、結び立ちに直る。	⑦のまま。	⑦のまま。
Pulling left foot then right foot, return to Musubidachi.	Same as in ⑦.	Same as in ⑦.
両手は開いて軽く添える。		⑦のまま。
Open both hands and place them lightly no thighs.		Same as in ⑦.
	礼をする。	
	Rei (Bow)	

チントウ
CHINTO

特徴

軽快かつ敏捷な形で、立ち方の種類も多く、その立ち方の変化は即ち体位の変化を表している。従って「緩急」「力の強弱」「重心の安定」が特に要求される形の一つである。

CHINTO is a nimble and agile KATA having various types of stance and its alteration signifies a variety of posture. Consequently, CHINTO is one of the types required to exhibit "quick and slow motion", "strength and weakness of power" and "balance of gravity".

チントウの立ち方

①（用意の姿勢から）右足を左足の後方に引き、両足先はほぼ南西を向き、前後の足幅は軽い四股立ち程度。
②体をすこし落とし、両脚をごくわずかに内輪にして立つ。ほぼ真半身になる。

Stance of CHINTO

①(from posture yo-i) Pull right foot toward back of left foot with both toes pointing almost southwest. Width between feet is about that of narrow Shikodachi.
②Lower body slightly, bend both legs slightly inward to be almost Ma-hanmi.

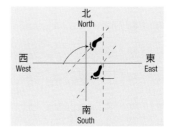

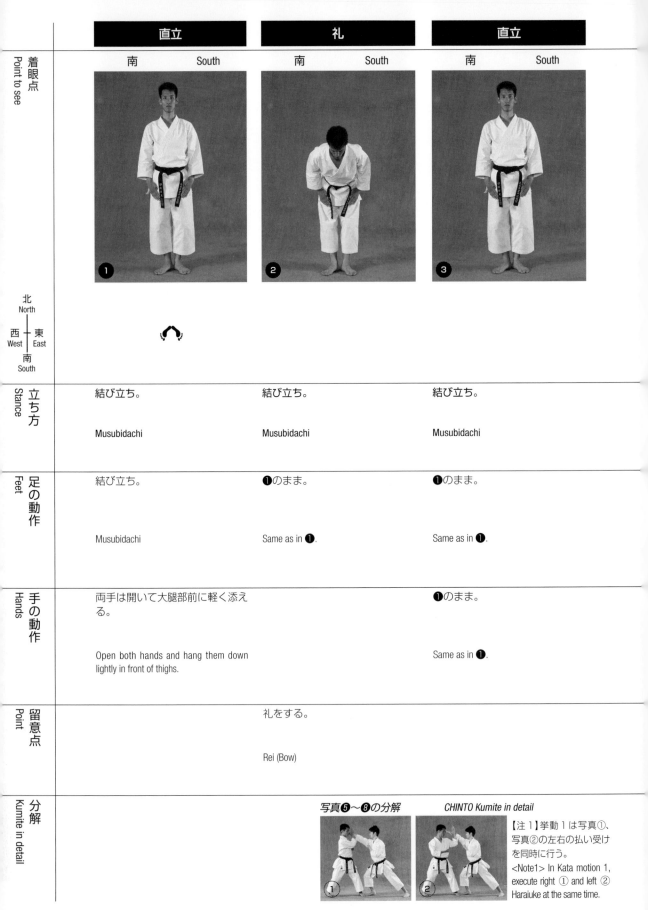

用意	1 挙動	2 挙動
南　　　South	南　　　South	南　　　South

	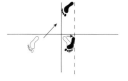	
八字立ち。 Hachijidachi	両踵は縦一線上にあり、両脚をやや内輪にする。歩幅は軽い四股立ち程度で斜め平行に立つ。 Keeping both heels on the same vertical line, turn both feet slightly inwards. Width of the stance should be the same as a narrow Shikodachi, with feet kept diagonally parallel to each other.	❺のまま。 Same as in ❺.
結び立ちより足を左、右と開き、八字立ちとなる（両踵の間隔は1足長半）。 Open left foot, then right foot from Musubidachi. Then, Hachijidachi (Width between heels is a foot and half apart).	右足を左足の後ろに引き、両足先を南西に向け、体はほぼ真半身にする。 Pull back right foot to behind left foot, with both feet pointng Southwest. The body should be facing almost sideways (Mahanmi).	❺のまま。 Same as in ❺.
両手は大腿部前で軽く握る。 Grip both hands lightly in front of thighs.	右手掌面、左手背面で同時に上段払い受けをする（右手が内側となり、両手首付近で交差する）。 Execute Jyodan-Haraiuke with right palm and back of left hand at the same time (cross both hands at aboutt wrists right hand inside).	両手で同時に中段打ち落しをする（左手が上で掌面下向き、右手下で掌面上向き）。 Execute Chudan-Uchiotoshi by both hands at the same time with left hand (palm facing downward) on right hand (palm facing upward).
	両手を同時に動作するが、左右別々の受けの動作を同時にするのである。 Move both hands at the same time, while each hand executes different Uke motion.	中段落し受けは両脇を締め右腕が水平に左脇腹を受ける。 Chudan-Otoshiuke is to defend toward left side of the body by horizontal right arm.

写真③：右手刀の甲面側前膊で左脇を打ち落し受けをする。
写真④：（その場で）相手の中段突きを左掌面側の前膊で打ち落し受けをする。

③Block his further Right -Chudantsuki by Uchiotoshi-Uke with wrist part of back of Right -Shuto.
④ (in the same position) Block his Right -Chudantsuki by Uchiotoshi with wrist part of left palm.

【注2】挙動2は写真③、写真④の受けの動作を同時に行う。

<Note2>In Kata motion 2, execute right ③ and left ④ Uke at the same time.

	3 挙動	4 挙動	
着眼点 / Point to see	南 South	南 South	途中
立ち方 / Stance	❺のまま。 Same as in ❺.	左縦セイシャン立ち。 Left-Tate-Seishandachi	左片足で立つ。 Stand on left foot.
足の動作 / Feet	❺のまま。 Same as in ❺.	右足を軸に、腰を左にひねって縦セイシャンの足になり、内輪に立つ。 Pivoting on right foot, twist body toward left to become Tate-Seisyan feet with toes pointing inward.	後ろからの蹴込みに対し、右足を引き上げてはずす（左足を軸とする）。 Against kick from behind, lift right foot to dodge it (put weight on left foot).
手の動作 / Hands	左拳中段突きをし、右拳は体側に引く。 Execute Chudantsuki with left fist and pull back right fist to right side of body.	右拳中段逆突きをし、左拳は体側に引く。 Execute Chudan-Gyakutsuki with right fist and pull back left fist to left side of body.	右肘を曲げ、右拳は右耳横に上げ、左拳は引いたまま。 Bending right elbow, lift right fist beside right ear, while holding left fist in the same position.
留意点 / Point	❺〜❽連続技として行う。 ❺ - ❽ All Performances will be judged as a continuous technique.	腰の回転が十分な突きで縦セイシャン立ちを正確に。 【備考】1〜4挙動まで連続して行う。 Tsuki with an adequate hips turn and Tate-Seishandachi precisely. <Note>Motion 1 - 4 must be executed in a continuos movement.	

分解 / Kumite in detail

形では3挙動、4挙動の動作を連続で行う。

In the Kata, movements 3 and 4 are executed in combination.

【注3】受け、または払いを行った後、ただちに攻め（突き、または蹴り等）をするのが原則であるが、形においては受け、払いののちの攻めを省略する場合が多い。

<Note3>Generally, it is the rule to counter-attack (with Tsuki, Keri, etc.) immediately after Uke or Harai. However, in Kata, attacks after Uke or Harai are apt to be omitted.

5 挙動

北 North	北 North	南 South

左片足立ち。	四股立ち。	左前屈立ち（順突きの足）。
Stand on left foot.	Shikodachi	Left-Zenkutsudachi
右足を左足前に回し、体を左転する。	右足を（左回りに）北へ運び、四股立ちになる。	右足を軸に、腰を左にひねり南を向き、順突きの足となる。
Bring right foot in front of left foot and turn body to left.	Turn body to left and put down left foot toward north, then, Shikodachi.	Pivoting on right foot, twist hips to left facing south, ten Jyuntsuki feet position.
❾のまま。	右下段払いをする。左拳は引いたまま。	右手内側、左手外側に交差する。
Same as in ❾.	Right-Gedanbarai. Left fist remains the same.	Cross both arms with right arm inside.

後足を引き上げたとき、立ち上ったり、流し受けの肘を高く上げたりしてはならない。回るとき中心軸がぶれないこと。

When back foot is raised, don't stand up nor raise high Nagashiuke elbow. When the body turns, axis must not be blurred.

写真❽～⓫の分解　　CHINTO Kumite in detail

		6 挙動	7 挙動	
着眼点 Point to see		南　　　　South	南　　　　South	南　　　　South 途中
		⑭	⑮	⑯
立ち方 Stance		左前屈立ち（順突きの足）。 Left-Zenkutsudachi	左前屈立ち（順突きの足）。 Left-Zenkutsudachi	空中。 In the air.
足の動作 Feet		⑬のまま。 Same as in ⑬.	⑬のまま。 Same as in ⑬.	南へ跳び、二段蹴りの右前蹴りをなす。 Jumping toward south, execute Right-Maegeri as fist part of Nidangeri.
手の動作 Hands		両手刀尺骨側で上段受けをする。 Execute Jyodanuke with ulna sides of both Shuto.	両手刀を正拳にし、尺骨側で左右同時に中段打ち落し受けをする（右拳上、左拳下に交差する）。 Change both Shuto to Seiken (fist) and execute Chudan-Uchiotoshi-Uke with ulna sides of both fists at the same time (cross both arms with right arm on top).	両拳は両胸前に構えながら。 Hold both fists in front of chest.
留意点 Point				
分解 Kumite in detail				

210　チントウ　CHINTO

8 挙動

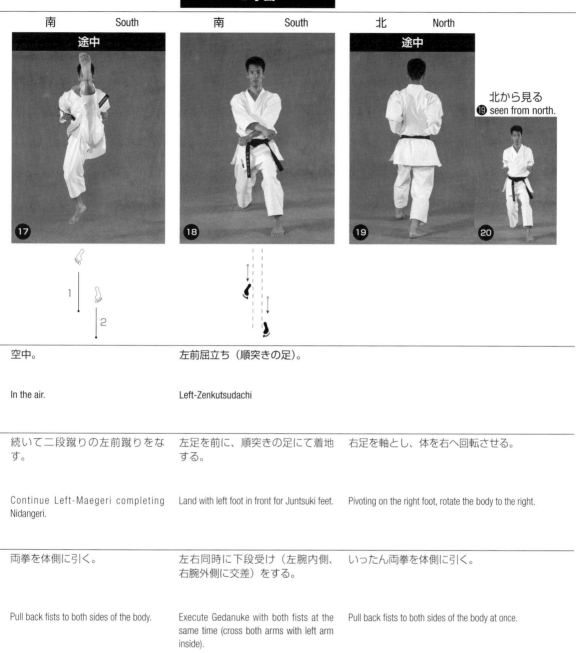

南 / South	南 / South	北 / North

空中。

In the air.

左前屈立ち（順突きの足）。

Left-Zenkutsudachi

続いて二段蹴りの左前蹴りをなす。

Continue Left-Maegeri completing Nidangeri.

左足を前に、順突きの足にて着地する。

Land with left foot in front for Juntsuki feet.

右足を軸とし、体を右へ回転させる。

Pivoting on the right foot, rotate the body to the right.

両拳を体側に引く。

Pull back fists to both sides of the body.

左右同時に下段受け（左腕内側、右腕外側に交差）をする。

Execute Gedanuke with both fists at the same time (cross both arms with left arm inside).

いったん両拳を体側に引く。

Pull back fists to both sides of the body at once.

	9挙動	10挙動	
着眼点 Point to see	北 North 北から見る ㉑ seen from north. ㉑ ㉒	南 South ㉓	南 South 途中 ㉔
立ち方 Stance	左前屈立ち（順突きの足）。 Left-Zenkutsudachi	左後屈立ち（右膝を伸ばす）。 Left-Kokutsudachi (stretch right knee).	右足で立ち、左足を軽く引きつけ。 Standing on right foot, pull left foot together lightly.
足の動作 Feet	左足を北に運ぶ。 Move the left foot toward North	左足を軸とし、体を右転し、左膝をやや曲げ、右脚は伸ばして、体を北に傾倒させる（後ろからの上段突きを引き込み流す動作）。 Pivoting on left foot, turn body to right, then bend left knee slightly and stretch right leg. Lean upper body toward north (as motion for slipping away from Jyoudantsuki from behind).	右足を軸に、左足を右足に引きつけ、いったん体をまっすぐに起こしながら。 While pulling left foot to right foot, raise body straight up at once.
手の動作 Hands	足が極まると同時に、左右下段受け（左腕内側、右腕外側に交差）をする。 As soon as setting feet, execute left and Right-Gedanuke (cross both arms with left arm inside).	右拳は下段構え、左拳は胸前に構え。 Gedangamae with right fist. Hold left fist in front of chest.	両拳を手刀にし、左手は胸前に右手はそのまま下段に構えながら。 Positioning left hand in front of the chest and keeping right hand as it is at Gedan, open both hands into Shuto.
留意点 Point			
分解 Kumite in detail		写真㉓〜㉕の分解 	CHINTO Kumite in detail  注．下段構えは相手の攻撃を受け払う動作に応用変化できる。 Note:Gedangamae would be applied for Ukebarai against opponent's attack.

212　チントウ　CHINTO

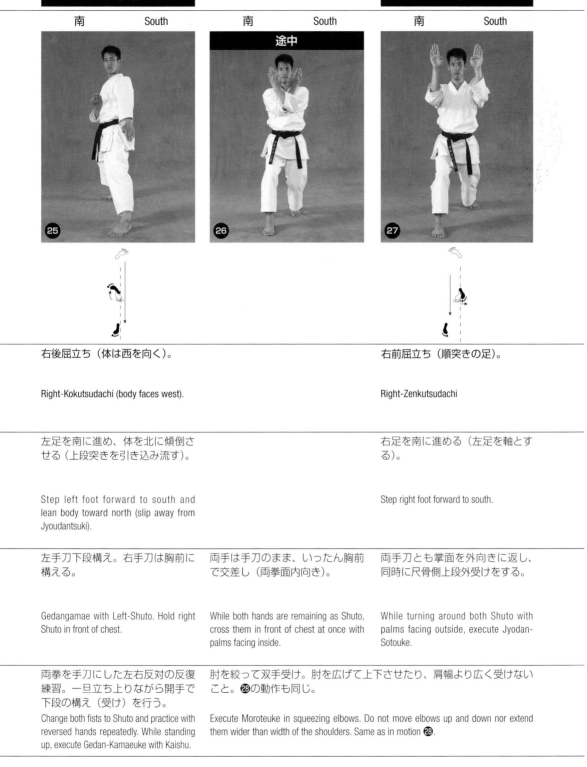

11 挙動 — South

右後屈立ち（体は西を向く）。

Right-Kokutsudachi (body faces west).

左足を南に進め、体を北に傾倒させる（上段突きを引き込み流す）。

Step left foot forward to south and lean body toward north (slip away from Jyoudantsuki).

左手刀下段構え。右手刀は胸前に構える。

Gedangamae with Left-Shuto. Hold right Shuto in front of chest.

両拳を手刀にした左右反対の反復練習。一旦立ち上がりながら開手で下段の構え（受け）を行う。

Change both fists to Shuto and practice with reversed hands repeatedly. While standing up, execute Gedan-Kamaeuke with Kaishu.

（途中）

両手は手刀のまま、いったん胸前で交差し（両拳面内向き）。

While both hands are remaining as Shuto, cross them in front of chest at once with palms facing inside.

肘を絞って双手受け。肘を広げて上下させたり、肩幅より広く受けないこと。㉙の動作も同じ。

Execute Moroteuke in squeezing elbows. Do not move elbows up and down nor extend them wider than width of the shoulders. Same as in motion ㉙.

---

12 挙動 — South

右前屈立ち（順突きの足）。

Right-Zenkutsudachi

右足を南に進める（左足を軸とする）。

Step right foot forward to south.

両手刀とも掌面を外向きに返し、同時に尺骨側上段外受けをする。

While turning around both Shuto with palms facing outside, execute Jyodan-Sotouke.

213

	13 挙動	14 挙動	15 挙動
着眼点 Point to see	東　　East	北　　North	北　　North　　東から見る ㉚ seen from east.
立ち方 Stance	狭い四股立ち。 Narrow Shikodachi.	狭い四股立ちの足幅。 Standing narrow Shikodachi.	右後屈立ち（左膝を伸ばす）。 Right-Kokutsudachi (stretch left knee).
足の動作 Feet	右足を軸に、体を左転して東に向け、左足をやや西に移して狭い四股立ちとなる。 Pivoting on right foot, turn body to left facing east and bring left foot slightly toward west to become narrow Shikodachi.	足はそのまま、両膝を伸ばして顔は北に向ける。 Without changing foot position, stretch both knees and turn face toward north.	左足を北に進め、体を南に傾倒させる（左方からの上段突きを引き込み流す）。 Step left foot forward to north and lean body toward south (slip away from Jyodantsuki from left side).
手の動作 Hands	両手刀のまま、右腕外側、左腕内側に交差し、両掌面を内向きに返し、両橈骨側上段外受けをする。 While both hands are remaining as Shuto, cross them with right arm outside, then, turn around them with palm facing inside. Execute Jyodan-Sotouke with radius sides of both Shuto.	両手は握りながらおろす。 While clenching hands, pull them down.	左拳下段構え、右拳は上段構えをする。 Gedangamae with left fist and Jyodangamae with right fist.
留意点 Point			
分解 Kumite in detail	写真㉘〜㉚の分解　　CHINTO Kumite in detail		

16 挙動

北　　　　North	北　　　　North	南　　　　South
途中	途中	途中
㉜	㉝	㉞

左足に右足を引きつけ。	左後屈立ち（右膝を伸ばす）。	右足に左足を引きつけ（両足先はほぼ南を向く）。
Pull right foot to left foot together.	Left-Kokutsudachi (stretch rigth knee).	Pull left foot to right foot (toes pointing almost toward south).
左足を軸に、右足を左足に引きつけつつ、体をいったんまっすぐに起こしながら。	右足を北に進め、体を南に傾倒させる。	右足を軸に、体を後ろ回りに（左回転）しながら左足を引きつけ、いったん体をまっすぐに起こし、顔は一瞬南を向く（左右に相手を想定して動作する）。
While pulling right foot to left foot, raise body straight up at once.	Step right foot forward to north and lean body toward south.	Pivot on right foot. Pull left foot turning body back around to left, then, raise body straight up at once. Face to south briefly (as if preparing to move against opponent on left and right).
左右の構えは柔らかに。	右拳下段構え、左拳上段構えをする。	左右の構えは柔らかに。
Kamae with both hands must be supple.	*Gedangamae with right fist and Jyodangamae with left fist.*	Kamae with both hands must be supple.
		一旦立ち上がり、相手を意識しながら次の動作の方向に目線を向ける。北と南に相手を仮想し、南をふり向きながら南の相手を見つめ、次の瞬間、北からの上段攻撃を引き込み流す。
		While standing up, pay attention to next movement direction imaging opponent's of south and north. Looking back toward south, look at eyes of opponent. Next moment, slip away from Jyodan attack of another opponent from north.

	17挙動		18挙動
着眼点 Point to see	北　North	東　East	東　East
	③⑤	途中 ③⑥	③⑦
立ち方 Stance	右後屈立ち（左膝を伸ばす）。 Right-Kokutsudachi (stretch left knee).	右足爪先立ち。 Right- Tsumasakidachi.	右足爪先立ち。 Right- Tsumasakidachi.
足の動作 Feet	体を左転して左足を北に進め、体を南に傾倒させる（顔は北を向き、体は東向きとなる）。 Turning body to left, step left foot forward to north and lean body toward south (facing north, but body faces east).	左足の真後ろに、右足を爪先立ちにして運ぶ。 Bring right foot just behind left foot standing on tips of toe.	足はそのままに、体を低く沈める。 Without changing position on feet, lower body further more.
手の動作 Hands	左拳下段構え、右拳上段構えをする。 Gedangamae with left fist and Jyodangamae with right fist.	両拳はいったん体側に構えながら。 Hold both fists on lower side of the body at once.	左右同時に下段受け（左腕内側、右腕外側に交差）をする。 Gedan-Uke with both fists at the same time (cross both arms with right arm on top).
留意点 Point	【備考】15挙動の形に同じ。 <Note>Same as in motion 15.		腰を曲げて下段受けをしないようにする。体の重心は両足の中心にとり、左足のみにかけないこと。 Don't defend by Gedan-Uke with bending upper body. Weight should be put between both feet. Don't put weight only on left foot.
分解 Kumite in detail			

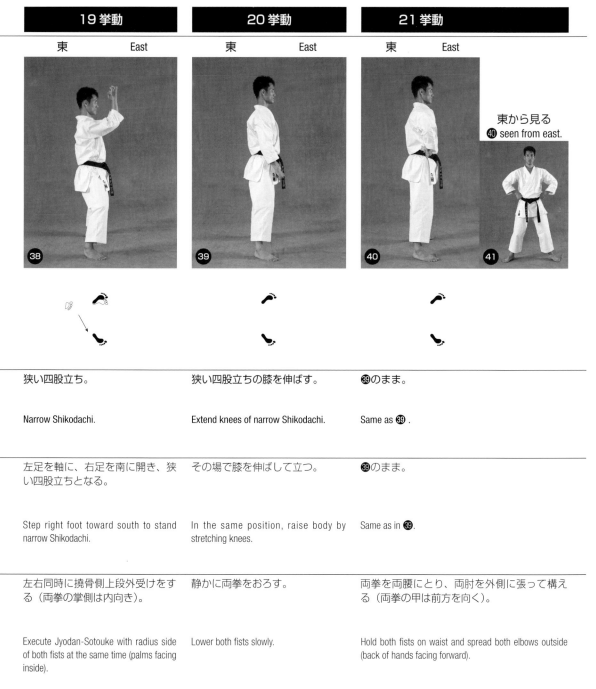

19 挙動	20 挙動	21 挙動
東 East	東 East	東 East
狭い四股立ち。	狭い四股立ちの膝を伸ばす。	㊴のまま。
Narrow Shikodachi.	Extend knees of narrow Shikodachi.	Same as ㊴.
左足を軸に、右足を南に開き、狭い四股立ちとなる。	その場で膝を伸ばして立つ。	㊴のまま。
Step right foot toward south to stand narrow Shikodachi.	In the same position, raise body by stretching knees.	Same as in ㊴.
左右同時に橈骨側上段外受けをする（両拳の掌側は内向き）。	静かに両拳をおろす。	両拳を両腰にとり、両肘を外側に張って構える（両拳の甲は前方を向く）。
Execute Jyodan-Sotouke with radius side of both fists at the same time (palms facing inside).	Lower both fists slowly.	Hold both fists on waist and spread both elbows outside (back of hands facing forward).

	22 挙動	23 挙動	24 挙動
着眼点 Point to see	東　　　East	東　　　East	西　　　West
立ち方 Stance			右足の後ろ左脇に、左足爪先立ちになる。 Bringing the left foot to the inside of the right leg, stand in left Tsumasakidachi (Left foot on tiptoe).
足の動作 Feet	狭い四股立ちの膝を軽く曲げる。その場で、体を落としながら、腰を左にひねる。 From a narrow Shikodachi, slightly bend the knees. Keeping on the spot, drop bodyweight and twist waist to the left.	その場で、体を右にひねる。 In the same position, twist hips to right.	右足を軸に、右回りして後ろを向き（西を向く）、左足を右足の後ろ左脇に運ぶ。 Pivoting on the right foot, rotate to the right to face behind (West). Move the left leg to the inside rear side of the right leg.
手の動作 Hands	前方からの中段突きに対し、右肘受けをする。左拳はそのまま。 Block Chudantsuki from front with Right -Hijiuke. Left fist remains the same.	左中段肘受けをする。 Left-Chudan-Hijiuke.	両拳の撓骨側で同時に上段外受けをする。 Jyodan-Sotouke at radius sides of both fists at the same time.
留意点 Point	肘受けは腰の回転で行い、それに伴って足先も変化する。手首を曲げたり、膝を固くして上半身のみを使って行なうのは受けが不充分となる。 Hijiuke must be performed by hip turn, and then foot toe is moved. Executing with wrist only or upperbody only with stiff knee action will be an insufficient Uke.		【備考】手の形は 19 挙動に同じ。 <Note>Hands are same as in motion 19.
分解 Kumite in detail			

218　チントウ　CHINTO

南　South

途中

西から見る
㊺ seen from west.

右片足で立つ。

Stand on right foot.

右足を軸とし、顔を左（南）に向けると同時に、左足を上げて左足が右膝後ろに軽く触れるようにする（相手が左足を払ってくるのをかわす）。

Pivoting on right foot, turn face to the left (South), at the same time lifting left foot so that it lightly contacts the back of right knee (evading opponent's attack against left foot).

顔を左（南）に向けると同時に、左拳は左側方下段に払い、右拳は右側方上段に構える。

While turning face toward left (south), hold left fist at Gedan on left side and right fist at Jyodan on right side.

南　South

途中

西から見る
㊼ seen from west.

㊺のまま。

Stand on right foot.

㊺のまま。

Same as in ㊺.

右拳は体側に引き、左前膊は胸前に平行に構えて、両拳を右胸側に構える（右拳下、左拳上に軽く触れ合う程度）。

Pull right arm to right side of the body and put left arm horizontally in front of chest, placing both fists on right chest (both fists touching lightly, with left fist on top).

㊺〜(51)連続動作。片足立ちとなり下段の構え（又は払い）と上段の構えが同時、中段の払いと蹴りを同時に行うがこのときのリズムと引き拳、蹴りの引足が不充分な場合次の突きが弱くなる。一連の動作として評価する。

㊺ - (51) Continuous movement. While standing on one foot, Gedankamae (harai) and Jyodankamae must be executed simultaneously. However, insufficient of the strength of rhythmical movement and Hikiken and Hikiashi in kick action will debiliate next Tsuki. These movements will be judged as a continuous movement.

		25挙動
着眼点 Point to see	南 South 途中  49 西から見る ㊾ seen from west.  50	南 South  (51)
北 North 西 West 東 East 南 South		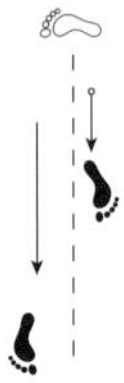
立ち方 Stance	㊺のまま。 Stand on right foot.	右順突き立ち（前屈立ちの足）。 Right-Zenkutsudachi
足の動作 Feet	左横蹴り（上足底）をなす。 Left-Yokogeri (Josokute).	左足を南におろし、右足を南に 1 歩進める。 Put down left foot toward south and take right foot one step toward south.
手の動作 Hands	相手の中段突きを左拳で横に払うと同時に、左横蹴りをする。右拳は引いたまま。 While brushing sideways opponent's Chudantsuki with left fist, execute Left-Yokogeri. Right fist remains the same.	右中段順突きをする。左拳は体側に引く。 Right-Chudan-Juntsuki. Pull back left fist to left side of body.
留意点 Point		
分解 Kumite in detail	*写真㊺～㊾の分解*　　*CHINTO Kumite in detail* 	

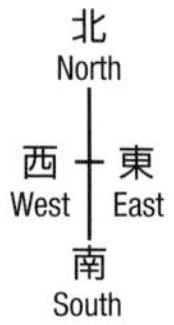

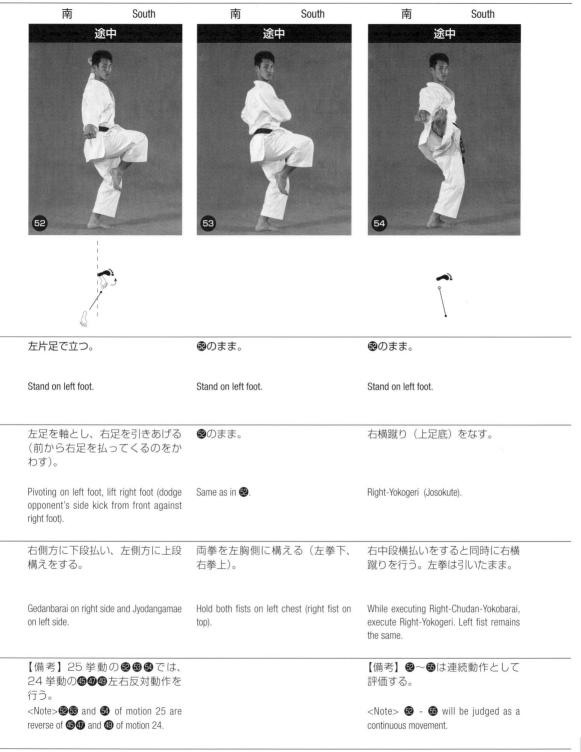

南　　　South	南　　　South	南　　　South
途中 ㊾	途中 ㊿	途中 ⓾
左片足で立つ。	㊿のまま。	㊿のまま。
Stand on left foot.	Stand on left foot.	Stand on left foot.
左足を軸とし、右足を引きあげる（前から右足を払ってくるのをかわす）。	㊿のまま。	右横蹴り（上足底）をなす。
Pivoting on left foot, lift right foot (dodge opponent's side kick from front against right foot).	Same as in ㊿.	Right-Yokogeri (Josokute).
右側方に下段払い、左側方に上段構えをする。	両拳を左胸側に構える（左拳下、右拳上）。	右中段横払いをすると同時に右横蹴りを行う。左拳は引いたまま。
Gedanbarai on right side and Jyodangamae on left side.	Hold both fists on left chest (right fist on top).	While executing Right-Chudan-Yokobarai, execute Right-Yokogeri. Left fist remains the same.
【備考】25 挙動の㊿⓾⓾では、24 挙動の㊺㊼㊾左右反対動作を行う。 <Note> ㊿⓾ and ⓾ of motion 25 are reverse of ㊺㊼ and ㊾ of motion 24.		【備考】㊿〜⓾は連続動作として評価する。 <Note> ㊿ - ⓾ will be judged as a continuous movement.

	26 挙動		
着眼点 Point to see	南　South	北　North 途中	北　North 途中
	55	56	57
立ち方 Stance	右縦セイシャン立ち。 Right-Tate-Seishandachi (wide stance).	右片足で立つ。 Stand on right foot.	56のまま。 Standing on right foot.
足の動作 Feet	右足を南におろし、縦セイシャン立ちになる。 Put down right foot toward south to become Tate-Seishandachi.	後ろから左足を払ってくるのを、左足を引きあげてかわす。 Lift left foot to dodge opponent's side kick from behind.	56のまま。 Same as in 56.
手の動作 Hands	左中段逆突きをする。右拳は体側に引く。 Left-Chudan-Gyakutsuki. Pull back right fist to right side of body.	後ろをふり向きざま、左側方下段払い、右側上段構えをする。 As soon as turning around, take Gedanbarai on left side and Jyodangamae on right side.	両拳を右胸側に構える（右拳下、左拳上）。 Hold both fists on right chest (left fist on top).
留意点 Point	腰を充分ひねって逆突きの縦セイシャン立ちとなる。 Perform Tate-Seishandachi for Gyakutsuki by twisting hips sufficiently.		
分解 Kumite in detail			

北 North
西 West ― 東 East
南 South

222　チントウ　CHINTO

27 挙動

北　　　　North	北　　　　North	南　　　　South
途中		途中
⑤⑧	⑤⑨	⑥⓪

⑤⑥のまま。	左縦セイシャン立ち。	四股立ち。
Stand on right foot.	Left-Tate-Seishandachi	Shikodachi
左横蹴り（上足底）をする。	左足を北におろし、縦セイシャン立ちになる。	左足を軸に、体を右転し、南に四股立ちとなる。
Left-Yokogeri (Josokute).	Put down left foot toward north to become Tate-Seishandachi.	Pivoting on left foot, turn body to right to become Shikodachi toward south.
左中段横払いをすると同時に、左横蹴りを行う。右拳は引いたまま。	右中段逆突きをする。左拳は体側に引く。	南をふり向きざま、右手を開く。
While executing Left-Chudan-Yokobarai, execute Left-Yokogeri. Right fist remains the same.	Right-Chudan-Gyakutsuki. Pull back left fist to left side of body.	Turn to face South, opening right hand.

223

		28 挙動	29 挙動	30 挙動
着眼点 Point to see		南　　　　South	南　　　　South	南　　　　South
		東から見る ❻❶ seen from east. 61 62	63	64
立ち方 Stance		四股立ち。 Shikodachi	右縦セイシャン立ち。 Right-Tate-Seishandachi	右縦セイシャン立ち。 Right-Tate-Seishandachi
足の動作 Feet		❻❶のまま。 Same as in ❻❶.	左足を軸とし、腰を右にひねり、右足をわずかに右に開き、南に縦セイシャンの足になる。 Pivoting on left foot twist hips to right and step right foot slightly toward right to become Tate-Seishandachi toward south.	❻❸のまま。 Same as in ❻❸.
手の動作 Hands		尺骨側で右中段懸け手受け、右手首の尺骨側で懸ける（手首を外屈させてつかむ）形にする。左拳は引いたまま。 Right-Chudan-Kakete-Uke. Shape the wrist and hand as if grabbing the opponent's forearm (bend the wrist outwards and grab). Keep the left arm pulled in.	左肘を立てて、下から突き上げるように、中段に左縦肘当て（右掌面に当てる）をする。 Hold left elbow up and attack toward Chudan with left elbow as if hitting upward (hitting against right plan).	腰のひねりをすこしもどし、左手を手刀にし指先を下方に向けて左腰横に構え、その掌面に右拳を甲面下向きに軽く添える。 Returning twisted hips a little, change left fist to Shuto and hold it on left hip with fingers pointing downward, while placing right fist on it lightly with back of hand facing downward.
留意点 Point		中段懸け手受けの肘が体側外に出て斜めに受けないこと。❻❶は❻❶を極める途中の動作。 At Chudan-Kakete-Uke, elbows must not come out of the body and defend diagonally. Motion of ❻❶ is in the process of performing ❻❶.	肘当ては肩より高くならないで縦セイシャン立ちとなる。次に左腰に構える拳はスピーディに構える。 Hijiate must be performed at Tate-Seishandachi so that Hijiate performance is not higher height than shoulder. Succeeding fist holding at left hip must be done quickly.	
分解 Kumite in detail		写真❺❾〜❻❸の分解　　CHINTO Kumite in detail		

224　チントウ　CHINTO

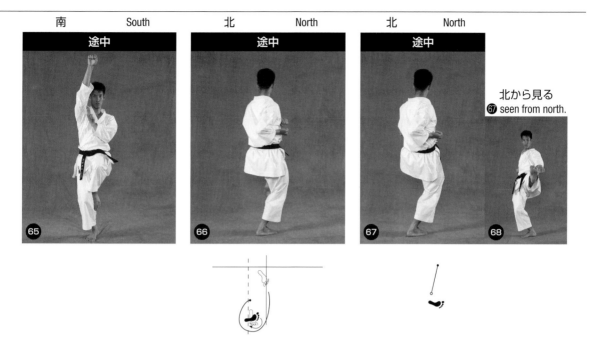

南　　　South	北　　　North	北　　　North
途中	途中	途中

北から見る
❻❼ seen from north.

右片足で立つ。	右に180°回転し、右片足で立つ。	❻❻のまま。
Stand on right foot.	Turning right 180 degrees, stand on right foot.	Stand on right foot (Same as in ❻❻).
後ろから左足を払ってくるのに対し、左足を引きあげてかわすと同時に前蹴りの構えをする。右足を軸とする。	右足を軸とし（右拳で掬いあげ打った調子に乗って）体を右に回転させ、後ろ（北）を向く。	左中段前蹴り（上足底）をする。
While lifting left foot to dodge opponent's kick from behind, take Maegerigamae.	Pivoting on right foot, turn body to right facing backward (toward north).	Execute Left-Chudan-Maegeri (Josokute).
右裏拳で相手の鼻を掬い打ち、左手刀は胸前に構える。	体を右転し、北に向いて軽い左半身程度となり、両拳を右胸側に構える（右拳下、左拳上）。	左中段横払いと同時に左足で蹴りをする。右拳は体側に引いたまま。
Execute Right-Uraken-Sukuiuchi to the opponent's nose, and position left hand in Shuto in front of the chest.	Turning body to right, face toward north to become light left Hanmi with both fists on right chest side (with left fist top and right fist below).	Execute Left-Chudan-Yokobarai and left kick at the same time. Keep the right fist held at the side of the body.
バランスを取ろうとして裏拳打ちを斜め横に打たないようにしなければならない。		中段横払いと蹴りは同時に行うが右の引手がゆるんではならない。
Do not execute Uraken-Uchi diagonally in order to keep balance of movement.		Chudan-Yokobarai and kick must be performed simultaneously and must not loosen right Hikite.

写真❻❹～❻❺の分解　　CHINTO Kumite in detail

225

	31 挙動	止め	直立
着眼点 Point to see	北　North 北から見る ⑥⑨ seen from north. ⑥⑨ ⑦⑩	南　South ⑦①	南　South ⑦②
立ち方 Stance	右順突き立ち（前屈立ちの足）。 Right-Zenkutsudachi	八字立ち。 Hachijidachi	結び立ち。 Musubidachi
足の動作 Feet	左足を北におろし、右足を北に1歩進める。 Put down left foot toward north and take right foot one step toward north.	右足を軸に、体を左に回転させて後ろ（南）向きになり、左足を右足の東に引いて用意の姿勢にもどる。 Pivoting on right foot turn around body to left with face backward (south), then, pull left foot to east of right foot. Thus return to Yo-i posture.	足を左、右ともどし、結び立ちに直る。 Pull left foot then right foot to return to Musubidachi.
手の動作 Hands	右中段順突きをする。左拳は体側に引く。 Right-Chudan-Juntsuki. Pull back left fist to left side of body.	両手をそれぞれ大腿部前におろす。 Lower both hands in front of thighs.	両手は開いて軽く添える。 Open both hands and place them lightly no thighs.
留意点 Point	【備考】⑥⑤～⑥⑨は連続動作として評価する。 <Note> ⑥⑤ - ⑥⑨ will be judged as continuous movement.	止め、直立も、残心に留意する。 Pay attentions to Zanshin at Yame and Naore.	
分解 Kumite in detail			

226　チントウ　CHINTO

礼	直立
南　　　　South	南　　　　South
 ⑦③	 ⑦④

結び立ち。	結び立ち。
Musubidachi	Musubidachi

⑫のまま。	⑫のまま。
Same as in ⑫.	Same as in ⑫.

	⑫のまま。
	Same as in ⑫.

礼をする。	
Rei (Bow)	

監修

■（公財）全日本空手道連盟　中央技術委員会　教範作成小委員会

栗原茂夫	SHIGEO KURIHARA
阪梨　學	MANABU SAKANASHI
佐藤重徳	SHIGENORI SATO
原口髙司	TAKASHI HARAGUCHI
村松真孝	MASATAKA MURAMATSU
前田利明	TOSHIAKI MAEDA
岩田源三	GENZO IWATA
香川政夫	MASAO KAGAWA

演武者

【サイファ・セーパイ】

宮崎健太　　KENTA MIYAZAKI

【ジオン・カンクウダイ】

在本幸司　　KOJI ARIMOTO

【バッサイダイ・セイエンチン】

大木　格　　ITARU OKI

【セイシャン・チントウ】

伊藤祥太　　SHOTA ITO

演武協力者

【サイファ・セーパイ】

西山　走　　KAKERU NISHIYAMA

【ジオン・カンクウダイ】

林田至史　　CHIKASHI HAYASHIDA

【バッサイダイ・セイエンチン】

荻原昌志　　MASASHI OGIHARA

【セイシャン・チントウ】

大島　翼　　TSUBASA OSHIMA

空手道形教範　第一指定形

2017年10月19日　改訂版第一刷

編集　　公益財団法人全日本空手道連盟　中央技術委員会
編者　　公益財団法人全日本空手道連盟
発行　　株式会社チャンプ
　　　　〒166-0003　東京都杉並区高円寺南4-19-3 総和第二ビル
　　　　電話：03-3315-3190（営業部）

©Japan Karatedo Federation 2017
Printed in Japan　印刷：シナノ印刷株式会社

定価はカバーに表示してあります。
乱丁・落丁本は、ご面倒ですが(株) チャンプ宛にご送付ください。送料小社負担にてお取り替えいたします。

ISBN978-4-86344-018-0